Emerging Dynamics in Audiences' Consumption of Trans-Media Products

Emerging Dynamics in Audiences' Consumption of Trans-Media Products

The Cases of *Mad Men* and *Game of Thrones* as a Comparative Study between Italy and New Zealand

Carmen Spanò

ANTHEM PRESS

Anthem Press
An imprint of Wimbledon Publishing Company
www.anthempress.com

This edition first published in UK and USA 2022
by ANTHEM PRESS
75–76 Blackfriars Road, London SE1 8HA, UK
or PO Box 9779, London SW19 7ZG, UK
and
244 Madison Ave #116, New York, NY 10016, USA

First published in the UK and USA by Anthem Press in 2021

British Library Cataloguing-in-Publication Data
A catalogue record for this book is available from the British Library.

Library of Congress Control Number: 2020940786

ISBN-13: 978-1-83998-542-3 (Pbk)
ISBN-10: 1-83998-542-9 (Pbk)

This title is also available as an e-book.

CONTENTS

Chapter 1

INTRODUCTION

A COMPLEX MEDIA LANDSCAPE

Television as a traditional medium has been changing for a number of years due to the development of a complex scenario characterized by the growing proliferation of platforms across which multiple forms of media are deeply interconnected. In this multimodal environment, traditional and modern media platforms have started to combine, revolutionizing both the technology and the manner in which audiences engage with media content of interest. Indeed, the progressive digitization of media content and the fragmentation of television delivery and reception have been affecting the ways in which media are accessed and consumed, to the point that "the construction of textual boundaries has shifted from producers to media consumers" (Sandvoss, "Reception" 246). Audiences operate as active users of media content by exercising control over their viewing schedules, and by integrating the media texts they are interested in into their lives through new patterns of consumption. This freedom in the modes of accessing and engaging with diversified media material has also benefited from the development of trans-media storytelling. The expression refers to the increasingly popular delivery of related media content across a set of media platforms, resulting in a particular "narrative structure that expands through both different languages (verbal, iconic, etc.) and media (cinema, comics, television, video games, etc.)" (Scolari 587). Movies, games, TV series, novels, webisodes, podcasts, comic books, fan fiction and many other media forms all come together in creating a rich, expanded story-world. In his seminal work *Convergence Culture* (2006), Henry Jenkins asserts:

> A trans-media story unfolds across multiple media platforms with each new text making a distinctive and valuable contribution to the whole. In the ideal form of trans-media storytelling, each medium does what it does best—so that a story might be introduced in a film, expanded through television, novels, and comics; its world might be explored

through game play or experienced as an amusement park attraction.
(Jenkins 95–96)

Elizabeth Evans, who in 2011 carried out a study on audience engagement
with online and mobile phone content related to the TV shows *Spooks* and *24*,
defines the same concept as "the increasingly popular industrial practice of
using multiple media technologies to present information concerning a single
fictional world through a range of textual forms" (Evans, *Transmedia Television*
1). The word "industrial" is important here. In the current mediascape rich
in on-demand content, trans-media emerges as "one of the most widespread
strategies of media corporations" (Scolari 590) for engaging audiences because
it optimizes the transformation of imaginary worlds into expanded narrative
brands. Brands represent "complex discourse universes with a strong narrative
imprint" (Scolari 599).[1] The aim of the increasing transformation of TV series
into fictional worlds is to build a solid relationship between the brand and the
consumers by matching the brand's values with consumers' lifestyles.

According to Nele Simons, "the television industry has been experimenting
with new ways to secure its central position in the media landscape" (2221)
in order to gain viewers' attention and devotion. Indeed, the proliferation of
distributors and delivery platforms as well as viewers sharing content translates,
among other things, into an ever more divided attention span on the part
of audiences. One way to overcome this diffusion is to generate "emotional
investment" (Askwith 3). Henry Jenkins has defined this strategy in terms of
"affective economics," or "a marketing logic that seeks to understand the emotional underpinnings of consumers' decision making as a driving force behind
viewing and purchasing decisions" (Simons 2221). The concept of brands as
virtual worlds in which individuals can immerse themselves constitutes the
driving logic according to which the majority of today's media conglomerates
choose to promote and sell their products and services. Trans-media storytelling
plays a substantial role in the achievement of this task since it "introduces a
mutation in this scenario in which the brand is no longer inside the fiction, but
rather the fiction *is* the brand" (Scolari 599). Characters, topics, aesthetic style,
costumes, settings—all these fictional attributes contribute to the foundation
of enhanced narratives whose specific traits can be transported across multiple platforms with the intent of offering a wide set of experiences. Audiences
become actively involved in the exploration of these universes, mainly because
they feel more free to select the best options—in terms of timeframe, contexts

---

[1] See also Codeluppi, 2000, 2001; Ferraro, *La pubblicità nell'era di Internet* and "Entrare nel
www"; Semprini, *Lo sguardo semiotico* and *La marca dal prodotto al mercato, dal mercato a la
società*; Semprini and Musso.

and device choices—for consuming media products. Trans-media texts, therefore, represent a useful tool for exploring the dynamics of today's audience practices.

However, it is important to keep in mind that old media forms still exist and have not been removed from the actual contexts in which both producers and consumers operate:

> A vast number of media products are still produced by media corporations, which are old top-down systems based on capitalist logics and not always in favor of the maximalist approaches toward participation and democracy. (Carpentier, *Media and participation* 207)

This means that media convergence becomes a field of struggle between old media conglomerates and empowered consumers, whose freedom in participating and creatively managing the media texts they come in contact with is not totally free from hindrances and restraints. The main intent in the building of fictional worlds that can be freely navigated by fans is to provide forms of engaged consumption whose directions can, eventually, still be regulated and exploited by media conglomerates. These limitations help media companies to exert a significant amount of control on the ways their products can be used and appropriated by industrious consumers, and they also represent the lens through which the ongoing shift in the audience's role has to be valued and understood.

To argue that audiences have become an essential part of the media production system means that their actions weigh more in today's media environment, and are taken into greater account by media companies. Indeed, audience members are offered various opportunities to manage their time in relation to the consumption of TV products, as well as to distribute their creative productions. Nonetheless, it is necessary to ask, is there a limit imposed on this freedom? Do media producers succeed in steering audiences' consumption habits? And if they do, are audiences aware of this condition that aims to monitor their activities and take advantage of their creative works? As Terranova observes, "free labor is the moment where this knowledgeable consumption of culture is translated into productive activities that are pleasurably embraced and at the same time often shamelessly exploited" (37).[2] It

---

[2] With regard to the results of this investigation, the concept of "free labour," which describes fans who are both willing and able to produce creative works related to the object of interest, comes out as a practice that pertains to a minority group of individuals, that is, to highly passionate and devoted followers who can be considered as highly invested fans. This being said, it is worth noting the significance of this type of production as a grassroots initiative. Indeed, fans' "free labour" is mainly for others fans' sake and, from

is in the balance between the embrace and exploitation of cultural products that originate from audiences' "free labor" that the complexity of the current media scenario lies. Therefore, a proper examination of audiences' behaviors in responding to the consumption options offered by trans-media franchises is indispensable for understanding audiences' effective role in this cultural production circuit, as well as in the social and technological transformations of our times. In turn, these consumption practices also relate to and influence audience members' sense of identity. As something under constant (re)construction, identity is affected by the daily experiences of making decisions, engaging with the world and reflecting on one's own actions. The consumption of and investment in television programs have become a significant part of this set of everyday experiences, to the point that they affect individuals' identities as well as their social relations.

The objective of this research project is to investigate the new forms of empowered agency possessed by audiences with reference to two particular television texts: *Game of Thrones* and *Mad Men*. The two popular American TV shows are highly successful products of the convergence era, which "is marked by trans-media storytelling in which reception practices of a text within one medium need to be analyzed in relation to the inter-textual and inter-medial contexts of such a text" (Sandvoss, "Reception" 246). Much has already been written about the significance of trans-mediality in relation to the Hollywood context, with scholars examining forms of trans-media intertextuality (Kinder), trans-media storytelling (Jenkins, *Convergence Culture*; Evans, *Transmedia Television*) and trans-media story-worlds (Scolari; Wolf), and others investigating the relation of trans-media to fandom (Hills, "The Expertise"; Bennet and Booth) as well as models of trans-media brand advertising (Tenderich and Williams; Freeman). This research has, so far, mainly focused on trans-media narratives and story-worlds, with the main goal being to conceptualize the central characteristics of the phenomenon, rather than to focus on actual audience practices. Multiple media platforms used by participatory audiences, however, call for new studies and theorizations.

The analysis of audience engagement with trans-media texts will disclose important information about the various ways people organize their lives around media as well as on how these activities help them to make sense of the world they live in. As Sandvoss has noted, "the moment that the single text as a recognizable and identifiable category seems increasingly to disappear in a converging media environment is hence precisely the moment when reception aesthetics becomes an essential methodological and conceptual tool in the

---

this perspective, it becomes effective as a means for intensifying both the interest and the investment of followers in general.

study of media audiences" ("Reception" 246). The investigation undertaken for this study has been structured as a comparative study between two distinct countries: Italy and New Zealand. These two countries have been chosen as reference contexts for the investigation of audiences' consumption behaviors because they represent nondominant media markets, both Anglophone and non-Anglophone, that remain to be properly studied and explored. Although they tend to be conflated in generic audience studies, national audiences represent strategic markets for the circulation of international fiction. In investigating the consumption modes that characterize the distribution of American television programs in these cultural contexts, the aim is to provide insights into the culturally specific similarities and differences that distinct audiences disclose in consuming the same texts.

TWO CASE STUDIES: *MAD MEN* AND *GAME OF THRONES*

Mad Men (AMC, 2007–15) and *Game of Thrones* (HBO, 2011–19) have been selected as case studies because they are substantial examples of trans-media narratives that "tell multiple stories over multiple platforms that together tell one big pervasive story, attracting audience engagement. It is not about offering the same content in different media platforms, but it is the world-building experience, unfolding content and generating the possibilities for the story to evolve with new and pertinent content" (Gambarato 4). The "world-building experience" is possible thanks to the employment of the core concepts of trans-media storytelling within the structure of the shows. During his talk at the *Futures of Entertainment Conference* at MIT in 2009, Henry Jenkins listed the following elements of trans-media narration: multiplicity, seriality, spreadability, drillability, immersion, extractability, world-building, performance.[3]

"Multiplicity" "allows fans to have access to alternate versions of characters or parallel universe version of the story" (Gambarato 6), whereas "seriality" involves "the notion of breaking up a narrative arc into multiple distinctive parts or installments not simply within a single medium, but rather spread out across multiple media systems" (7). Similarly, *Mad Men* and *Game of Thrones* present multiple entry points (via different media technologies) for their followers, and this circuit of extensive content allows followers to actively engage in a process of reconnection of the events and stories through which they can also manage to detect gaps and excesses in the narratives. The function of these discursive strategies is to keep audiences' thirst for more content and more explanations always alive, and at the same time to involve them in an endless,

---

[3] See Gambarato, 14–24. On this topic, see also Jenkins, "Revenge of the Origami Unicorn."

captivating discovery game. The opportunity that both shows give "to explore, in depth, the content of narrative extensions offered by a trans-media story" (Gambarato 6) is defined in terms of "drillability": drillable media stimulate spectators "to dig deeper, probing beneath the surface to understand the complexity of a story and its telling" (6). This experience usually affects the relationship between the trans-media worlds and the audience's everyday life, so that "a vertical descent into a text's complexities" implies one's "immersion" (Gambarato 6) into the fictional universe generated by the story. Apps, books, videogames, interactive features and online discussions populate the *Mad Men* and *Games of Thrones*' trans-media apparatuses and are all means to this end. On the other hand, "extractability" "refers to the possibility fans may have to take away with them aspects of the story, incorporating it in their everyday lives (e.g., memorabilia)" (Gambarato 6); *Mad Men* and *Game of Thrones*' extensive merchandise performs this exact function. In addition, "a trans-media story is indeed a story-world capable to support multiple characters and multiple narratives across multiple media. Trans-media extensions often lead to fan behavior of capturing as many elements of the story as possible" (7). In accordance with this concept, the world-building practice is a collaborative construction of "charts, maps and concordances" (Jenkins, "Revenge of the Origami Unicorn"), partly provided by producers (e.g., *Mad Men* summarizing videos, *Game of Thrones* genealogy lists) and partly created by fans themselves in order to fulfill their desire "to map and master as much as they can know about such universes" (Jenkins, "Revenge of the Origami Unicorn"). The production of user-generated content by fans and followers is another fundamental feature of trans-media, defined as "the ability of trans-media extensions to stimulate fans to produce their own performances that can become part of the trans-media narrative itself" (Gambarato 7). The so-called cosplay phenomenon,[4] for instance, is an interesting example of the creative activities in which viewers may engage by taking inspiration from the setting, the costumes and the accessories of their favorite TV program. In a similar way, *Mad Men* fashion contests and online guides for making cocktails and organizing fancy parties inspire spectators' creativity in finding their own direction in the re-creation of environments and ambience from the past.

In addition to the critical acclaim and complex structure that substantiate the prestige and the narrative quality of both *Mad Men* and *Game of Thrones*,

---

[4] "Cosplay" is a term that derives from the contraction of the words "costume" and "play." It refers to a practice in which participants, named "cosplayers," dress up in costumes and fashion accessories to represent a particular character from an imaginary universe. These reenactments are generally popular among fans of narratives that belong to the sci-fi or fantasy genre.

the two TV series exhibit other relevant attributes that make them exemplary case studies for this research project. First, the TV shows belong to different genres, with *Game of Thrones* developing as fantasy whereas *Mad Men* is a historical drama. This diversity in content, styles and depiction of historical periods (allowing for the fact that *Game of Thrones* is fantasy-history) calls attention to a variety of tastes and narrative preferences across a heterogeneous sample of viewers, an aspect considered fundamental to the effectiveness of focus group sessions. Indeed, research participants who describe distinct consumption behaviors can stimulate discussion on an extensive set of perspectives and experiences. Second, *Game of Thrones* and *Mad Men* originate from highly different production realities. The former is an HBO creation with a wide and extremely active international fan base (de Castella); the latter is produced by Lionsgate, broadcast by AMC and has a smaller group of loyal followers. In New Zealand, both shows are broadcast by SoHo, a premium entertainment channel available to subscribers on SKY Network television. In Italy, *Mad Men* is broadcast by the free thematic channel Rai4, which, in the multichannel Italian landscape, targets a niche audience with specific tastes for movies and TV programs. *Game of Thrones*, on the other hand, is available to subscribers on SKY Atlantic, a new channel of the SKY platform. These facets emphasize the diversity between the two shows in terms of reach and level of engagement.

METHODOLOGY

The methods employed for gathering useful data for the comparative analysis were both quantitative and qualitative. The first phase of data collection consisted in the production of four online surveys: two in the English and two in the Italian language. They were all implemented on the website SurveyMonkey.com (https://www.surveymonkey.com/home/). The Italian surveys were launched in late May 2015, since I planned to organize the qualitative phase of data production—the focus group discussions—in Italy for the following months of June and July 2015. As for the English surveys that addressed the New Zealand fans of the series, those were launched at the end of August 2015 and the first focus group with New Zealand fans of *Game of Thrones* took place in September 2015. In order to distribute the surveys, I contacted many Italian and New Zealand websites and blogs dedicated to both the shows: the *Game of Thrones*/*Mad Men* Facebook pages; the New Zealand blogs Flicks.co.nz, Throng and The Spinoff; the discussion list MediaNZ (medianz@lists.otago.ac.nz); the Italian movie and TV series website *Mediacritica* (http://www.mediacritica.it); the Facebook page of Rai4, the national network channel that airs the dubbed versions of the series in

Italy; the website *Cinefilos* (https://www.cinefilos.it); and a popular site of
Italian subtitled media that allows viewers to stream the shows' episodes online
in English with Italian subtitles, *Italiansubs* (https://www.italiansubs.net). The
managers of these sites expressed their interest in my research, and agreed to
post the links to the surveys. The questions in the surveys were the same for
both shows (with the exceptions of a couple referring to specific lists of items/
games/applications related to each series), with the overall aim being (a) to
gain initial insights on fans' consumption trends; (b) to acquire a general sense
of the main reasons for fans' passion for the shows and (c) to select potential
participants for the focus group sessions.[5]

As to the first aim of better understanding fans' consumption trends,
questions 1 to 6 focused on the investigation of fans' modes of viewing the
series as a main activity. Questions 7 and 8 centered on the possible activities
being carried out in parallel to the viewing process, in particular those that
refer to the potential interaction with other people (respondents were asked
to choose from a provided list of options). These two questions were instrumental to acquiring a general sense of the degree of attention manifested
by viewers in watching the shows, and of the significance of social interaction as part of a process related to the series themselves. Questions 9 to 16
focused on fans' tendency to produce and distribute original material (user-
generated content) related to the shows, and on fans' level of interest in the
media extensions that constitute the trans-media apparatus of both the TV
programs (questions 15 and 16 only appeared in the *Game of Thrones* surveys
since they specifically refer to George R. R. Martin's novels). As for the main
reasons for fans' passion for the shows, an open-ended question at the end
of the first section of the survey provided respondents with the possibility to
explain, in their own words, the reasons for their appreciation of the shows,
as well as to leave personal comments on aspects and issues regarded by them
as important and significant. The second section of the surveys consisted of
nonidentifying, demographic questions about the respondents themselves.
The inquiries helped to delineate a general profile of the target audiences
of both series in terms of gender, age range, education and occupation. The
last question in this section represented a first step in the recruitment process of potential participants for the subsequent phase of data collection, the
focus groups. In Italy, the survey on *Game of Thrones* registered the participation of 863 people, whereas the one on *Mad Men* collected 153 responses in
total. As for New Zealand, the questionnaire on *Game of Thrones* received 202
responses, and the one on *Mad Men* 43.

---

[5] A complete transcription of the questions from the surveys can be found in Appendix I:
Survey Questions.

The second phase of data production consisted of the organization of the focus group sessions. Focus groups have long been used to identify consumer behaviors and motivations: "The primary aim of a focus group is to describe and understand meanings and interpretations of a select group of people to gain an understanding of a specific issue from the perspective of the participants of the group" (Liamputtong 3). This qualitative approach is considered ideal for "examining the stories, experiences, points of view, beliefs, needs and concerns of individuals" (5) with regard to the social processes of communication. Furthermore, this methodology is regarded as a useful tool "to generate rich, believable data" (Lunt and Livingstone 92). The first two focus groups took place in June 2015 with the Italian fans of *Game of Thrones*; in the month of July I organized the other two sessions with the Italian fans of *Mad Men*. The focus groups were conducted at Università Cattolica del Sacro Cuore in Milan. Participants were recruited through the online surveys, through live announcements that I delivered in front of university students, and through word of mouth (fans asked other fans they knew if they were willing to take part in the initiative). Each group was composed of 10 individuals and the discussion lasted for about two hours; it took place in the late afternoon, after work hours. Each session was recorded, transcribed and translated into English by myself afterward. I followed the same procedure in order to recruit people in New Zealand for the focus groups that I organized in Auckland, after the field research in Italy was completed.[6] A few survey respondents expressed their interest in participating in the group meetings; others learned about the project through my announcements during various lectures at the University of Auckland, while others were informed by their friends and decided to participate. The focus groups in Auckland with fans of *Game of Thrones* took place in September 2015 and March 2016, while the focus groups with New Zealand fans of *Mad Men* took place in Auckland in September and November 2016.

I started the group sessions with fans of *Game of Thrones* by showing participants a humorous video about one of the main characters of the show, Jon Snow (https://www.youtube.com/watch?v=BabsgCQhpu4). This helped to create a relaxed atmosphere in the room, which made participants more willing to start talking without the embarrassment or the fear of saying something wrong. During the moderation, I asked participants questions ranging

---

[6] The composition of the *Game of Thrones* fan groups was quite diverse from the *Mad Men* ones. For both nationalities, the former groups were composed of individuals in their 30s and younger, whereas in the latter groups individuals aged 40–50 turned out to be a significant presence. This fact was predictable in terms of the distinct audiences that *Game of Thrones* and *Mad Men* target, respectively.

from their viewing practices and habits to activities related to the series, such as their participation in both live and online discussions, the production and/or distribution of both original and reworked media material, the attendance of cosplay performances. Before asking direct questions on the show's content (the main characteristics of the plot, participants' opinions about the characters, the reasons for the shows' success, etc.), I showed a second video of fans' reactions to the unexpected death of one of the protagonists (Jon Snow again: https://www.youtube.com/watch?v=rEXdXKQP-r8). This video helped me to set up a discussion about the idea of "being a fan," a concept I asked participants about both in terms of personal perception (why they consider themselves as fans) and their perception of others. In the focus groups on *Mad Men*, I followed a similar procedure in terms of the questions that I chose to ask and their relevance to the main themes of the study (the mode of viewing, the engagement with the series' trans-media apparatus and the tendency to produce/distribute original content, the storylines and the characters' profiles), but I obviously employed different videos at the beginning and at the middle of the sessions. I started by showing a *Mad Men* tribute video: https://www.youtube.com/watch?v=bt2EzCODIL8, once again to create a comfortable environment so that people would feel that they were about to engage in a conversation about a topic they enjoyed and were interested in. The other videos that I showed participants were instrumental in directing the discussion toward the series' storylines and characters' attributes, and they were both chosen from the first season of the show:

https://www.youtube.com/watch?v=VPs7dAMFkPM (Don and Rachel dialogue, S01E01)
https://www.youtube.com/watch?v=suRDUFpsHus (The "Carousel" Pitch, S01E13).

Chapter 2

RETHINKING AUDIENCES IN A TRANS-MEDIA, TRANSNATIONAL AGE

What does it mean to be "an audience"? From the original idea of audience established in ancient societies to the modern notions that take into account the dynamics through which people come together into groups as well as the development of new forms of spectatorship, the term has been employed with different nuances. What is interesting to observe is the increase in complexity that has affected the definition of the word over the years. In this chapter, I approach the changes in the meaning of the term as being strictly dependent on the historical contexts in which the word has been employed. This overview is instrumental to the research project, as it provides the theoretical basis upon which the project is built, and helps to explain my project's contribution to scholarship.

In the first section, I provide a brief introduction to the evolution of audience theories and explain why it is still necessary to study audiences today; the transformations in audience configuration and behaviors become symptomatic of the social and cultural changes that apply to modern societies at a general level. In "The Concept of the Audience," I present a more detailed discussion of the ways in which the idea of audience has been conceptualized at different stages. I refer to the initial idea of audience as synonymous with passive individuals who are powerless under the harmful influence of mass media (media effects theory) and, subsequently, to the modern theories about audience members and their acknowledged capacity to approach media texts from a critical perspective (interpretation theory and audience reception studies). The theoretical framework of the audience as composed of active users who are able to interpret and use media texts is outlined in the next section, through the presentation of the main studies that have examined the nature of audience agency in consuming media programs. "Audiences and New Media" extends this perspective on audiences to discuss the significance of audience practices in the contemporary era. At this point, the concept of "convergence culture" (Jenkins, *Convergence Culture* 2) provides my argument with the cultural and technological background that allows me to explain the significant transformations in the current media landscape, as relevant to audience practices. In particular, the diffusion of trans-media storytelling as a widespread media corporate strategy to retain audience interest and the revaluation of fans' roles and works in the circuit of cultural production and distribution are examined with reference to this complex paradigm shift. In this regard, the changes in the television text and the notion of *produser* are fundamental to understanding the implications and the directions of development in the relationship between old media producers and new users of media. The last section illustrates how these theories have led me to include the importance of cultural specificity when it comes to audience behaviors, both in the delineation of my research questions and in the choice of the appropriate methodology.

THE IMPORTANCE OF RESEARCHING AUDIENCES

During the first half of the twentieth century, the audience represented a community of individuals who were seen as uncritical recipients of messages. Nico Carpentier traces this to the role of the audience as simple "receivers": "The passive model of the actor has a long history, and is present in one of the most stubborn communication models in the history of communication studies: the sender-message-receiver model of Shannon and Weaver (1949)" ("New Configurations of the Audience?" 192). This was also the basis for media effects theory, "which is mainly inspired by the concern and/or fear for the disadvantageous effects that the media might have on the receiver(s)—usually articulated as potential victims—in a number of specific fields" (Carpentier, "New Configurations of the Audience?" 192). This theory was profoundly connected to the diffusion of propaganda during the Second World War. Subsequent studies embraced and developed the idea of a smarter and more aware consumer, who was capable of selecting among media entertainment forms as a source of personal gratification. In 1980, Stuart Hall, who established the Centre for Contemporary Cultural Studies at the University of Birmingham, wrote a revolutionary essay on the ability of audience members to interpret messages, and texts in general, in an active way, according to their own beliefs and social or class backgrounds. Hall's essay on encoding/decoding provided evidence of the practices adopted by individuals during their encounters with media texts, and marked the inception of a new approach to audience studies. The acknowledgment of audience agency has led scholars to observe more in depth the range of audience practices in different contexts (like the home), and with regard to different groups (family, community of fans, society). Meanwhile, developments in technology have led to a multiplication of the screens—portable and of varied sizes—as well as of the ways, both legal and illegal, through which to gain access to media content. More recently, the traditional, industrially upheld boundary between media producers and consumers has been breached. Increasing audience participation in the actual production of media texts has caused the rethinking of the dynamics and configurations of the producer–text–audience relationship. In the changing context, the term audience takes numerous forms and refuses simple classification or analysis. In *The Handbook of Media Audiences* (2011), Virginia Nightingale asserts, "So rather than the term *audience* disappearing, it seems to be attracting new modalities and expanding in relevance, and, even more importantly, revealing the specialization creeping into the generic term *new media user*" (7). And yet, even if the terminology is still unresolved, and even if tracking audiences has become more challenging in contexts that provide people with so many alternatives for media consumption, these are also the very reasons why studying and exploring audiences today is necessary: "the audience remains of key importance for media research, and particularly for understanding contemporary media's social consequences" (Couldry 213).

At this point, methodological questions emerge. Which approach can be regarded as the most suitable for investigating audiences in the twenty-first century? Which methods of analysis can help researchers to better understand the interweaving of personalized viewing practices, the involvement of fan communities with their favorite texts and the creative tension that energizes the dialectics between the system of old producers of media and the new *produsers* of content? The term *produser* was coined by Axel Bruns and has replaced Alvin Toffler's older term *prosumer*. Bruns explains the meaning of the word by arguing that

> the distinctions between producers and users of content have faded into comparative insignificance. In many of the spaces we encounter here, users are always already necessarily also producers of the shared knowledge base, regardless of whether they are aware of this role—they have become a new hybrid, *produser*. (Bruns 2)

Media encounters constitute an ever increasing aspect of people's lives. For this reason, it has become necessary to investigate the realities of the everyday experiences that people have with the media so as to understand how these complex processes affect their identities, social relations and the contexts in which they interact with one another.

THE CONCEPT OF THE AUDIENCE

James G. Webster has identified three main models of the media audience that summarize the different concepts mentioned above: "audience-as-mass," "audience-as-outcome" and "audience-as-agent." In the first model, audiences are regarded as "a large collection of people scattered across time and space who act autonomously and have little or no immediate knowledge of one another" (Webster 193). This concept grounds the modern notion of the audience as a loose collection of people that exists beyond the boundaries of physical space. The second model "sees people as being acted upon by media. Typically, it reflects a concern about the power of media to produce detrimental effects on individuals" (193). The media effects theory directly relates to this idea, since it considers individuals as basically powerless components of a collectivity in need of protection from the harmful influences of media messages. Finally, according to the "audience-as-agent" paradigm, "people are conceived of as free agents choosing what media they will consume, [...] generally using media to suit themselves" (194). The idea that people are not merely objects of media effects but, on the contrary, are able to exert direct control over the ways they consume media texts represents the fundamental assumption of audience research today. Active audience theories—the uses and gratification approach, the notion of audience interpretation and audience reception theory—have become progressively important in the scholarly literature since the 1970s. From that time on, the significance of audience agency in reading media texts and incorporating them into social environments has become central in researchers' studies. From David Morley to John Fiske, from Henry Jenkins to Carlos Alberto Scolari, the concept of audiences as active and even participatory users of media has been analyzed from multiple perspectives and through the adoption of different methods. It is evident from this condensed excursus that the act of conceptualizing the audience is central to the media sphere, since "audiences are seen not [only] as empirical actors to be examined in their concrete activity, but as discursive constructs. [...] To study audiences is to study the discourses that take audiences as their object" (Bratich 243).

AUDIENCES AS "ACTIVE USERS": INTERPRETATION THEORIES AND AUDIENCE RECEPTION STUDIES

The development of critical cultural studies during the 1980s represented a turning point in the definition of the audience's role in the process of media consumption. The basic assumption, following Stuart Hall, was that audiences showed the ability to interpret—or *decode*—different meanings. This theory of media interpretation originated from structural linguistics (namely, Ferdinand de Saussure's work), which explained the relation between signifiers and signifieds in terms of arbitrariness rather than as a natural, fixed connection. The principle implied that different signifiers could refer to different signifieds, or meanings; therefore, different interpretations of a sign—and, by extension, of a text—were not only possible but necessary. Hall drew on this theoretical frame to illustrate the dynamics of what he called the "two determining moments" in any communication process: encoding and decoding. As Jason Mittell explains, "According to this approach, the creation of media texts involves multiple meanings [...] texts are seen as encoded with multiple meanings through their production, rather than a singular sent message" (Mittell 363). Hall's pioneering essay influenced an entire generation of scholars and marked the beginning of the "first phase of reception studies," which "tended to focus on the interpretation of specific texts by structurally situated groups" (Sender 181). Sociologist David Morley set out to explore Hall's assumptions about audience decoding through his famous *Nationwide Study* (1980). Morley reported and analyzed audience responses to a weekly English TV show produced by the BBC, *Nationwide*. The participants were divided into four groups according to class since Morley, like Hall, believed that class plays a significant role in determining individuals' cultural beliefs and ways of thinking and acting. Morley aimed to comprehend which group of viewers would adopt which interpretive reading in watching the TV program. In the end, he found that individuals were able to make personal interpretations of media texts that were clearly influenced by their social positions. The *Nationwide Study* was a landmark in the first phase of audience reception studies.

Other scholars followed in Morley's footsteps and engaged in qualitative studies of the audience, notably Charlotte Brunsdon (1981), Dorothy Hobson (1982) and Ien Ang (1985), who used direct observation and interviews in their investigations. In addition to class distinctions, these researchers found that other elements such as race, gender and cultural context could also affect audiences' understanding of media programs. In particular, Ien Ang's study of Dutch female viewers of *Dallas* (the extremely popular American television program of the 1980s) revealed that women interpreted the show with a greater focus on the connotative level than the denotative one. Ang described two different ways through which female spectators enjoyed the show. According to the first modality, female fans showed a tendency to identify with the story and its melodramatic developments: "these viewers enjoyed being 'swept away' by the heightened, if not exaggerated, emotional highs and lows of the narrative" (Ang 5). In this case, what was perceived as authentic was the "tragic structure of the feeling" that made the emotions of the story so similar to real-life experiences. A different mode of viewing, on the other hand, was represented by a more detached position that allowed women to get pleasure from watching the program "while simultaneously expressing a confident knowingness about its supposedly 'low' quality" (5). Ang's investigation demonstrated that viewers do not interpret the same text in the same way. Moreover, Ang noted the national specificities of Dutch female fans in responding to this foreign text, even though her trailblazing work on nondominant national audiences of international programs was not picked up in most audience studies of the 1990s and 2000s.

The growing importance of the audience's role in the interpretation process was further conceptualized by John Fiske in his work *Television Culture* (1987). Fiske "emphasize[d] the social and negotiated aspects of meaning, in which meaning is interpreted as unstable (and always susceptible to reinterpretation) and contested" (Carpentier, "New Configurations of the Audience?" 192). He developed a concept of television that granted the audience decisive power in activating and completing the sense of media messages: "There is no text, there is no audience, there are only the processes of viewing" (Fiske 57). From this basic concept, Fiske derived the idea of television as a text with no fixed confines, which was at the same time polysemic because the structure of its storylines allowed for different understandings by different audiences. Furthermore, Liebes Tamar and Elihu Katz ("Patterns" and "Six interpretations") also referred to *Dallas* for their empirical research on media reception among distinct ethnic groups in Israel, and with American and Japanese viewers as well. The researchers found that television viewing was not generally an individual experience but a social engagement carried out with other people like family members and friends. The aim of their investigation was to understand to what extent spectators' cultural backgrounds and their social interactions could influence the reception of a television program. Katz and Liebes observed that audiences had a tendency to process texts through ideologies and codes that belonged to their own cultural backgrounds, as well as through the reference to other media texts. With regard to this aspect, Katz and Liebes's study constitutes a relevant precedent to researches that are conceived in the form of minority-nation analyses, even if not in a comparative form between distinct cultures, which is, instead, the approach adopted by the present study.

The process of building connections across distinct media experiences/ texts is called "intertextuality" and is described as "the fundamental and inescapable interdependence of all textual meaning upon the structures of meaning proposed by other texts" (Gray 4). The notion of intertextuality was borrowed by media scholars to explain the concept of interpretive community. According to the American scholar Stanley Fish, groups of readers and/or viewers can produce similar meanings of a text on the basis of shared tastes, experiences and life conditions. Like Fiske, Fish believed that authors and texts truly exist only when they are experienced by readers. In the end, all these studies provided evidence of the participatory role played by the audience in relating to media texts.

However, in Katz and Liebes's analysis the idea of culture as a factor that influences the audience's interpretation process was not fully explained. This was symptomatic of the need for a change of perspective that could take into account the specificities of consumption context(s) as well as the influence of multiple external factors on the viewing experience. Accordingly, audience reception research has taken as its main focus the specific context in which audience interpretation of media programs takes place. The term "context" identifies both a physical space and a network of relationships and interactions that happen within that space. It can be easily surmised that one of the most important spaces for the exploration of media reception processes is the home. The introduction of the television medium into this complex setting at the beginning of 1950s determined a reshaping of family communication dynamics. In the early 1980s, scholars started to scrutinize audiences in their domestic sphere of media consumption through the employment of research techniques such as participant observation and in-depth interviews. In *Family Television* (1986), David Morley moved beyond his own analysis of spectators' interpretations of a particular television text and decided to focus on "the social processes within which television viewing is enclosed" (Turner 144). Morley argued that "the changing patterns of television viewing could only be understood in the overall context of family leisure activity" (Morley 13). In conducting discussions with various families, Morley noted a substantial divergence between the way the home was considered by men and women. For men, the home was a space for relaxing and enjoying leisure time away from work at the end of the day, while for women the home was a workplace in which television viewing was mainly identified as a "guilty pleasure" instead of being a leisure pursuit. As a result, in *Family Television* Morley showed that the dynamics of audience reception within the home were connected to the difference in gender roles and to the patterns of communication that characterized the family itself. In this way, the study pointed out the presence of intersections between gender and contextual elements in the experience of watching television. Morley's later collaboration with Roger Silverstone and other affiliates in the Birmingham School started to give audience reception research a new direction. In an essay published in 1990, Morley and Silverstone wrote that the examination of television "requires a study of the domestic context within which audience's activities in relation to it are articulated and constrained" (Morley and Silverstone 34). In 1997, Sonia Livingstone conducted an important research on media use in the domestic context. She focused on English adolescents and their parents and discovered "a shift in media use from that of 'family television' to that of individualized media styles and, for children and young people, of 'bedroom culture'" (Livingstone 304).

Media practices in the home also represented the object of Stewart M. Hoover, Lynn Schofield Clark and Diane F. Alters's interview-based study. The scholars "were mindful of David Morley's interest in visiting domestic settings to see what people [...] do and say about the media" (Hoover et al. 6), and they, too, referred to previous analyses that focused on the understanding of household dynamics in relation to the consumption of media products. In particular, the authors' objective was to examine "how parents and children in different families deal with the gap between their practices and their accounts of the media" (5), basically in terms of the strategies that come into play when parents feel the need to exert influence over their children's use of media, and teenagers' response to this form of parental control consisting of specific rules and regulations.

The central idea was to provide insights into the process of identity construction within the domestic context in which media play an increasingly decisive role. This focus on identity as a process of self-realization is also highlighted in *The Makeover: Reality Television and Reflexive Audiences* (2012) by Katherine Sender, who describes identity as "not something that is just given [...] but something that has to be routinely created and sustained in the reflexive activities of the individual" (Sender 137). Hoover, Clark and Alters's analysis disclosed interesting points of observation with regard to how parents perceived themselves in relation to their role within a media-driven environment. The researchers were able to identify three modes of engagement with media texts for the members of the American families in their study. They named the first mode "experiences in the media," which consisted in "the diverse ways in which people said they experienced actual media texts" (70–71). The second mode, designated "interactions about the media," was instrumental in discerning "the way media texts were integrated into family life" (75). At this level, the study connects to the group of audience analyses that explored media-related interactions among family members as a means of spending valuable time together, and hence constructing and reinforcing the identity of the family as a unit, as in Morley's and Katz and Liebes's works. Finally, the third mode was named "accounts for the media," and referred to the various ways in which people managed to integrate media experiences into their existences, with a particular focus on the impact of these experiences on their identities, not only as single individuals but also with regard to the family context to which they belonged.

The findings about people's reflections on their own selfhood in media-situated contexts articulate with the disparate ways in which individuals interpret media programs and assimilate them in their lives. In today's media-saturated environment, however, these modes of engagement have increased substantially, and have produced a high level of complexity in the fabric of relations and media consumption. Elizabeth Evans's study of how audiences experience narratives through the use of multi-platform televisual technologies involved English viewers and their level of engagement with the TV drama series *Spooks* and *24*. Evans's conclusions about participants' consumption habits revealed their tendency to utilize multiple devices in watching the series' episodes: "computer or mobile phone can be transformed into 'television' or stand as technologies in their own right, depending on how the user engages with them" (*Transmedia Television* 175). Other research has examined, for instance, "how audiences navigate social networking sites like Facebook and Twitter" (Sullivan 247) and the reception of a multicultural Dutch soap opera, *Westside*, by using multiple methods like street interviews, focus group sessions, individual interviews and the analysis of discussions among fans on the official website of the program (see also: Das 343–60; and Muller and Hermes 193–208). In "Audience Reception of Cross- and Trans-media TV Drama in the Age of Convergence," Nele Simons's examination of how audiences make sense and take advantage of the opportunities offered by the television industry[1] had as its main goal to investigate audience interactions with the trans-media structure of sitcoms and soap operas. From a similar approach, Sarah Atkinson presented an analysis of the nature of "audience activity around *The Inside* as the manifestation of a *dramatic community*" (Simons 2201) in the United Kingdom. These recent studies indicate that the evolution in the concept of audience has to be understood with reference to the radical transformations effected by the processes of convergence culture, which have changed the technological and cultural architecture of society.

AUDIENCES AND NEW MEDIA

Convergence has become a crucial framework for understanding audience conduct and expectations since it represents more than just a technological change. In his foundational work, *Convergence Culture* (2006), Henry Jenkins explains that convergence "represents a paradigm shift—a move from medium-specific content toward content that flows across multiple media channels" (243). This mobility of content destabilizes the idea of television as a discrete object: its programs have become available on myriad platforms and in a wide range of narrative forms. It also undermines the classic idea of viewers as passive receivers of media texts. In 2008, Jay Rosen, in order to explain the implications of the novel ways through which audience members

---

[1] The study was conducted in Flanders, the northern Dutch-speaking region of Belgium.

participate in the circuit of production and distribution of fictional content, formulated the notion of "the people formerly known as the audience." He defined these people as "those who were on the receiving end of a media system that ran one way, in a broadcasting pattern [...] and who today are not in a situation like that at all" (Rosen 163). In today's media setting, spectators have the opportunity to watch their favorite programs at the time of their own choice and on multiple media platforms such as computers, videogame players, tablets, iPads, Kindles and so on. The act of consumption itself converts into a flux of practices that exceed the main activity of television viewing to include frequent online discussions, game sessions, streaming and/or downloading practices, offline meetings, the purchasing of items that resemble objects and characters from the show, the gathering and analysis of new information from numerous para-texts (i.e., books, comic novels, videos), the writing of fictional material and/or the production of user-generated content.[2] All of these interactive performances and activities are instrumental in involving audiences in an absorbing and potentially endless consumption circle: "there is now clearly an increased diversity of participatory practices supported by an increased availability of technologies" (Carpentier, "New Configurations of the Audience?" 199). Audiences utilize a wide range of devices that allow them to take advantage of numerous avenues through which to access the media content they are interested in, while also having the freedom to exert their power of choice in different spatial contexts, and at different times of the day. The practice of watching television has, therefore, gradually turned into a complex set of intertwined experiences that include a variety of roles for the participants, who find themselves absorbed—sometimes, even "lost"—in a continuous flow of media content and mediated encounters.

The concept of user-generated content reinforces the importance of audience activity in a domain that, in previous times, used to be perceived as a forbidden territory for those standing at the end of the consumption chain, but that in the present time has become progressively permeable. Alex Bruns employed the term *produser*[3] to signal the ongoing transformation in the relationship between the old media producers and the new empowered members of the audience. In *Spreadable Media*, Joshua Green and Henry Jenkins employ

---

[2] In its 2007 report, *Participative Web: User-Created Content*, the Organisation for Economic Co-operation and Development (OECD) explained user-generated content as the "certain amount of creative effort [that] was put into creating the work or adapting existing works to construct a new one" (Carpentier, "New Configurations of the Audience?" 198).

[3] The word has replaced Alvin Toffler's older term, *prosumer*. This use of terminology also highlights scholars' attempts to find more suitable terms to illustrate and explain the current media landscape and its mutations.

Bruns's notion as a starting point to explain how audience members today are using media content to build new connections with each other and to make sense of the world they live in: "audience members, both individually and collectively, exert agency in the spreadability model" (Green and Jenkins 123). Through the use of this model, Green and Jenkins enriched the terminology that is used to depict the current reality of multiple roles and relationships among players in the context of production and circulation of media material. They also illustrate the nature of consumers' participation in the Web 2.0 era by focusing on the relevance of their creative agency to the distribution of media content: "the spreadability paradigm assumes that compelling content will circulate through any and all available channels, moving us from peripheral awareness to active engagement" (118). The possibilities for literate users to direct media content along paths of consumption that differ from the official distribution channels are increased by the conjunction of people's improved technical skills and the existence of a large variety of technological tools employed for the exchange of media content. Scholars like Gerard Goggin have pointed out the relevance of mobile devices for consuming media programs: "new kinds of audience have been shaped around distinct and important new processes of engagement centering on the use of mobile devices" (Goggin 128). From its first appearance in the 1970s, the mobile phone has undergone significant modifications in its structure as a material object. Today smartphones and iPhones are something more than mere communication tools; indeed, they allow audiences to "use the mobile phone as a platform for cultural production and exchange, in ways reminiscent of the internet but also in ways that extend online culture" (Goggin 137). The new options for media engagement opened up by mobile devices constitute an additional challenge for audience researchers, since there is still much to understand about how, and to what extent, they influence audiences' behavior: "there is as yet little systematic work by researchers that draws together the various overlapping strands of going mobile and how it structures audiences" (Goggin 143).

The rise of these practices has been expedited by television itself, more specifically by the media companies that throughout the 1980s and the 1990s started to provide a new entertainment experience to their audiences. Television programs—and TV series in particular—began to develop into "multi-, cross-, and trans-media projects" (Caldwell, "Convergence Television" 50–53) whose narrative structures extend beyond the boundaries of the traditional medium. Jason Mittell describes this structure as follows:

> nearly every media property today offers some trans-media extensions, such as promotional websites, merchandise, or behind-the-scenes materials—these forms can be usefully categorized as para-texts in

relation to the core text, whether a feature film, videogame, or television series. (Mittell 293)

Henry Jenkins defines trans-media storytelling as "a process where integral elements of a fiction get dispersed systematically across multiple delivery channels for the purpose of creating a unified and coordinated entertainment experience" (Jenkins, *Convergence Culture*). This notion helps to explain the dynamics of consumers' immersion in fictional universes as a widespread strategy on the part of media companies aiming to create an alternative reality that permeates the time and space of everyday existence.

Media producers choose to conceive television stories according to this narrative technique because it helps in capturing and retaining audience attention by (a) offering a significant amount of content that consumers can interact with or can consume in different fashions and (b) transforming imaginary worlds into expanded narratives for consumers to explore and perceive as an all-encompassing experience. At the same time, trans-media storytelling represents a new place of negotiation between producers' original products and consumers' freedom in integrating them into their daily consumption routines. Henry Jenkins asserts:

> Both the commercial and grassroots expansion of narrative universes contribute to a new mode of storytelling, one which is based on an encyclopedic expanse of information which gets put together differently by each individual, as well as processed collectively by social networks and online knowledge communities. (Jenkins "Revenge of the Origami Unicorn")

With regard to Jenkins' definition of trans-media, it is necessary to point out the exact nature of the "unified and coordinated entertainment experience" conceived by the media scholar, as well as its implications in terms of media strategy and forms of engagement. Henry Jenkins's idea essentially refers to an enlarged structure made up of multiple entry points, via different media, in which *each constituent is equal to the others*. The consequence of this internal organization is the corresponding equality of consumers' experiences in pursuing the entertainment offered by the trans-media architecture. In Jenkins's model, each experience makes a unique contribution to the whole, thus adding to the creation of an inherently "democratic" distribution of means and opportunities for consumers. Ideally, this concept of trans-media functions in accordance to the basic paradigm of participatory culture. Nevertheless, in reality, trans-media systems are constructed and tend to work quite differently, as Jason Mittell points out in discussing their properties in *Complex TV: The Poetics of*

Contemporary Television Storytelling (2015). Mittell glosses Jenkins's notion in terms of what he calls "balanced" trans-media: a complex network of multiple nodes with no hierarchical structure, in which all elements contribute something of the same importance to the whole. In Mittell's words this represents the *ideal* model of trans-media storytelling, since, in reality, a significant number of trans-media systems are, in fact, "unbalanced": some elements of the structure emerge as more central and important than others. This fact implies the common existence of a hierarchy of texts in trans-media constructions, which, in turn, also involve a significant difference in the corresponding experiences pursued by consumers. This turns out to be a fundamental aspect in the dynamics that regulate trans-media as a strategy for generating interest and developing attachment, especially with reference to the results of the present investigation on the modes of audience involvement with the enhanced fictional universes of *Game of Thrones* and *Mad Men*.

The level of audiences' engagement with media texts has been scrutinized by researchers and analyzed by scholars in an attempt to understand the nature of the affection that ties the subject to his/her object of interest (or, in some cases, of obsession), and that tends to become a meaningful presence in the person's life. The intensification of branding across platforms demands that the notion of audience involvement with media texts is reassessed from the perspective of media convergence. For this reason, the evolution of the audience into the concepts of "fan" and "fandom work" are crucial to better frame the new dynamics that come into play in the relationship between traditional producers and empowered audience members.

AUDIENCES AND MEDIA FANDOM

Highly passionate audience members who demonstrate deep involvement through their engagement patterns have been labeled in the past as "fanatics." The word "fan"[4] originates directly from this term and, for quite a long time, it took upon itself the negative connotations of its etymological roots, that is, the idea of religious membership "of or belonging to the temple, a temple servant, a devotee" (Jenkins, *Textual Poachers* 12). Because

---

[4] The term "fan" appears to be quite controversial. In *Understanding Fandom* (2013), Mark Duffett refers to Harrington and Bielby's four-part model that explains fandom in terms of mode of reception, shared practice of interpretation, an "art world" of cultural activities and an "alternative social community" (*Soap Fans*, 96). Duffett also cites Henry Jenkins, who suggests that fandom includes five levels of activity: "a particular mode of reception, a set of critical interpretive practices, a base for consumer activism, a form of cultural production and an alternative social community" (*Textual Poachers* 277–80, quoted in Duffett 31).

of their singular tastes (which were usually oriented toward media programs and/or celebrities from popular culture) and their attitude in expressing these tastes, such individuals were perceived as a niche of atypical, fixated consumers who dwelled on the borders of mainstream culture, unrepresentative of the consumption trends that characterized audience behaviors. For this reason, they were positioned for quite a long time at the margins of the academic debate on cultural consumption. However, in 1992, in his book *Textual Poachers*, Henry Jenkins offered *Star Trek* fans the opportunity to speak for themselves, to explain in their own words the reasons for their passion and habits. Jenkins was able to demonstrate that the nature of fan involvement revealed an evident capacity for critical analysis. His work and that of other scholars like Camille Bacon-Smith advanced a new perspective on fans and their passions, and initiated a course of studies—called the "first wave of fan studies"—that shed a new light on these consumers and their relevance to the discourses on media consumption.

Fan engagement is characterized by "a particular emotional investment in a given popular text" (Sandvoss, *Fans: The Mirror of Consumption* 7) that involves specific patterns of consumption, and also by a strong and articulated capacity for analytical thinking. Fans are more than mere consumers; Sandvoss observes that "to see fandom as primarily about consumption is to forget that, first, fans often like things for free, and, second, that they are always more than consumers" (46). Fans can be both attached to and critical of the media texts they choose to incorporate in their lives. Through this process of constant analysis and investigation of the object(s) they are passionate about, fans tend to cultivate a personal sense of identity around the consumption of media texts. This attitude defies the negative stereotypes regarding the audience-as-mass (Webster 193) as being essentially passive and uncritical. Fandom is the term utilized to indicate "the social roles that [fans] inhabit" (Duffett 18). It identifies the set of practices through which fans express their tastes and passions, their sense of belonging to the fan community, their capacity to be self-reflexive about their identities and the ways they are affected by their consumption habits. These notions of self-reflexivity, shared values and critical discussion in relation to the act of media consumption gradually changed the way fans were perceived, because "to 'culturally' consume is to *meaningfully examine* a particular media product" (Duffett 20; emphasis as in original). In particular, the first wave of fan studies put emphasis on fans' modes of engagement as a form of resistance to the messages encoded in the texts by media institutions, and stressed the separation between producers on one side and fans on the other. The idea derived from Michel de Certeau's explanation of power relations as a context in which media producers' plans for control are, to some extent, counterbalanced by media users' strategies.

The first wave pursued the objective of recuperating those fan activities, such as "convention attendance, fan fiction writing, fanzine editing and collection, letter-writing campaigns" (Gray, Sandvoss and Harrington 3), which had previously been designated as detrimental by reframing them as artistic and productive. Nevertheless, the intricacy of roles, subjects and apparatuses in media systems extends beyond polar oppositions. This model represented the main limitation of these early studies, "which saw fans pinned into perennial battle against the power bloc" (6) by portraying fandom as a form of cultural opposition against the status quo. Subsequent studies on fandom shifted their theoretical focus from de Certeau's concept of power relations to Pierre Bourdieu's sociology of consumption. Bourdieu described the distribution and the preservation of power in society in more complex terms than de Certeau's binary model.

The "second wave of fan studies" (Dell; Harris and Alexander; Jancovich) considered fans and their communities as places where hierarchies can, to some extent, be preserved, and forms of exclusion can be reiterated; hence, fan communities can mirror—instead of opposing—power structures that belong to the dominant culture. Fans can discriminate, isolate and establish hierarchies within the fan groups they belong to. Scholars from the second wave focused on issues of intolerance and prejudice and did not regard fandom as a place of democratic acceptance; rather, they recognized in its manifestations the potential perpetuation of more extensive social inequalities. These Bourdieuian considerations provided a more accurate definition of fandom and popular culture by underlining the fact that they are not to be seen as "a priori" spaces of liberation. However, second-wave studies ran out of a valid rationale the moment their task of unmasking specific cultural beliefs within subcultures was accomplished. The question then arose, what about other important aspects—such as personal motivations, and the search for gratification—that affect fans' choices and behaviors, particularly with reference to the changing technological scenario that offers multiple forms of grouping and reorganization? Being a fan has become a common trait of modern consumption, and the various ways audience members who refer to themselves as fans experience their approaches to media content have undergone radical transformations.

The "third wave of fan studies" has taken into account this important shift, and has broadened the core of its investigation by focusing on the analysis of the self as something that is always under construction and is also shaped by the activities that are structured around media consumption. Furthermore, fans' habits and tastes are now considered as part of larger social and economic structures that are at the same time global and local (Harrington and Bielby, "Introduction: New Directions in Fan Studies"; Juluri 2003a, 2003b;

Sandvoss, *A Game of Two Halves*; Tufte). Since "fandom simultaneously encompasses both individual engagement and social participation" (Duffett 277), the significance of fans' activities as well as of their social interactions is determined by the realization that these practices have turned into an essential component of everyday life. Fandom as part of the texture of people's existence has become a valuable source of information about modern communication forms and the sociocultural dynamics of consumption. Cornel Sandvoss emphasizes the role of fandom in forging the identity of fans and how "it is, in every sense, a mirror of consumption" (*Fans: The Mirror of Consumption* 165). C. Lee Harrington and Denise Bielby situate the importance of fan studies within the theoretical framework of audience studies: "recent studies of fans and fandom force us to rethink key questions of identity, performance practice, genre, gender, sexuality, self, affect, race, ethnicity and nationalism" ("Introduction: New directions in fan studies," 799).

More than a matter of passion for a media object or a practice simplistically ascribed to the category of one's favorite hobbies, fandom reveals its relevance as a powerful tool in the building of identity and "in the positioning of one's self in the modern world" (Sandvoss, *Fans: The Mirror of Consumption* 165). To investigate fan audiences, therefore, can help scholars to understand the basic mechanisms according to which people think and behave in today's mediated environment because "fan audiences [...] tell us something about the way in which we relate to those around us, as well as the way we read the mediated texts that constitute an ever larger part of our horizon of experience" (Gray, Sandvoss and Harrington 10).

COMPARATIVE AUDIENCE STUDIES IN THE CONVERGENCE ERA

The current media landscape is in a state of notable transition. The convergence of media forms, described as "the flow of content across different media platforms, the migration of audiences and co-operation between different media industries" (Duffett 242) has generated a framework of intertwined technological and cultural practices. In this sense, the emergence of new strategies in the production and distribution of media content, as well as the evolution of audience behaviors, have radically altered the ways scholars used to explain the dynamics of media consumption and people's processes of identity construction. The scrutiny of how audiences are capable of handling the discrepancies—in terms of lifestyle portraits, prefabricated meanings and relevance of the media content distributed via multiple platforms—between their lives and the imposed values that are produced by mass culture is fundamental since media practices are ingrained in the daily routines of consumers' existence. In the present era, however, being an audience member is a condition in progress, consequently one yet to be properly delineated and understood. Mass media, and television in particular, provide audiences with chances of seeing and decoding the world—and these ways of watching in turn affect people's behaviors and relations. These developments have affected the nature of television as a traditional medium, both with reference to its fixed, stable presence in the living room of the households, and to its narrative systems of representation. We dwell in a media-saturated world: the multiplication of screens on which it is possible to watch media programs, in conjunction with the digitization of that content, have determined the fragmentation of television delivery and reception. Media are disseminated through a range of alternative platforms—generally smaller, portable and hence more relatable, like laptops, smartphones and/or tablets—and within a constellation of offers of additional content that has molded television stories out of expanded, branded universes. In this regard, the diffusion of trans-media storytelling as a tactic used by media conglomerates has provided the original cores of television programs like TV series with multiple entry points through which consumers can immerse themselves into imaginary worlds.

US TV programs like *Game of Thrones* and *Mad Men* represent notable examples of fictional stories that have been conceived in this way. Media texts in the guise of alternative worlds can be explored, but also rearranged and improved, by audience members. Fans are the privileged explorers of these imaginary universes since they "enter an emotionally significant relationship with mass-produced texts and commodities in which these come to function as extensions of the self. [...] fans are themselves shaped through their object of fandom" (Sandvoss, *Fans: The Mirror of Consumption* 164). In establishing this vital relation with media object(s), fans reveal themselves as "intense viewers of TV drama and early adopters of new TV and media technologies" (Simons 2225). Fans are a privileged source of information on the current ways in which individuals as consumers and *producers* of media content operate in the circuit of cultural consumption. In this regard, Mark Duffett states, "Fandom is about consumption *and* production, resistance *and* collusion. It reflects circulating assumptions, subjective feelings, shared experiences, common practices, imagined communities, collective values, social formations and group actions" (Duffett 288).

The interrelation of new media and audiences' demands has caused scholars to reconsider many of the traditional conceptions regarding media communication and cultural exchange. To what extent are people aware of the multiple venues of consumption they can take advantage of to engage with their favorite programs? If they are knowledgeable of these options, to what extent are they interested in them? What level of personalized viewing schedules do they tend to pursue? Which devices do they use most often and in which contexts? These types of questions are not redundant in an era in which divisions between production roles and consumption activities have become remarkably blurred. In "Spreadable Media," Joshua Green and Henry Jenkins underline the effects of audience agency on media producers' attitudes and ways of thinking: "Major commercial producers are having trouble adjusting their economic models to take advantage of alternatives to broadcast distribution, because they don't know how to value the work audiences perform when they are not simply 'consuming content'" (122–24). Nevertheless, Nico Carpentier notes that it is important to keep in mind that old media forms still exist and have not been removed from the actual contexts in which both producers and consumers operate: "A vast number of media products are still produced by media corporations, which are old top-down systems based on capitalist logics and not always in favor of the maximalist approaches toward participation and democracy" (*Media and Participation* 207). This means that audience freedom in creatively managing the media texts they come in contact with is not totally free from hindrances and restraints; these limitations help media companies to exert control on the ways their products can be used and altered by industrious consumers. The complex nature of this interweaving of practices, characterized by fluctuations in the relationship between conventional producers and active users, is worth investigating in the reality of its dynamics, by employing "an approach to audiences that is less media-centric and more open to the complexity of audience practice's embedding in social life" (Couldry 216). The analysis of the employment of different tools in the structuring of media activities can shed light in at least two ways: (a) on the literacy of audience members in concretely taking advantage of the technological and narrative apparatuses they are surrounded by, and hence on their actual participation in the process of media convergence and trans-media storytelling development; and (b) on the level of technological integration that individuals' modes of consumption reveal, with a particular focus on the use of devices in different contexts and their concrete influence on people's viewing habits. Most of the studies on audiences have referred to the North American context of media consumption. However, Liebes and Katz's cross-cultural reception analysis revealed that television viewing is a process made of negotiation phases that refer to the fictional story, the specific cultural background of the spectators and the communication exchanges among them. The audience did not act as a sponge that absorbs messages without questioning their internal sense of truth and significance. These mechanisms of meaning interpretation are amplified when producers of media messages and consumers belong to social contexts in which cultural codes and ideologies refer to a set of different and often clashing reference values.

In today's world, the global and the local are inevitably linked. Mass media have contributed extensively to the establishment of these social and cultural interconnections. Nevertheless, the political, social and cultural traits that still identify a nation—as different, in the eyes of its inhabitants, from any other country—constitute fundamental variables in the ways people think, behave and make sense of the world around them. For these reasons, audience researchers have progressively focused their attention on countries that are different from the United States. Countries that are nondominant media markets deserve particular attention from scholars and researchers, especially in an era that sees the dissemination of media programs all over the world. The analyses of these alternative contexts of media reception can provide useful insights into the consumption patterns of viewers who relate to media products that originate from distinct cultures. As Nick Couldry points out,

> What we lack and urgently need to develop are most international comparative studies of media culture and audience practices. There is every reason to expect that a comparative frame both within and between nations will disrupt our assumptions about the dominant forms of audience practice. We need […] a more open attention to the range of ways in which convergence may be working within societies (but between classes, genders, ethnic groups, and so on) and between societies. (226)

Moreover, Jonathan Gray highlights the importance of investigating fans' practices in relation to their sense of national belonging:

> There is still much work to be done in exploring the ways in which personal fandom has functioned in relation to nationality, family ties, ethnic affiliations and other components of social identity. […] more studies of fans in cultural contexts other than the English-speaking world may greatly enhance our understanding of fandom. (Gray, Sandvoss and Harrington 14)

Nondominant media markets like Italy and New Zealand, for instance, represent distinct contexts in terms of their sociocultural traditions, the expansion and usage of technology, and the policies that regulate distribution and access of online/mobile media contents. In Italy the development of the technological infrastructure and the progression of users' computer literacy have been happening at a different speed than in other European countries and, more pertinently, than in the United States (market of reference) and New Zealand (market of comparison). In this scenario, the aspect that is worth investigating is precisely the role and the attitude of Italian fans in approaching the media content they are interested in, so as to understand to what extent issues related to the development and the use of technology affect their choices in consuming the media extensions from the shows' fictional universes. Furthermore, all foreign media products are dubbed in Italy. This process requires time and creates a delay in the broadcasting of films and series on the official TV channels. This aspect has consequences on fans' behaviors with regard to the alternative sources they decide to look for in order to find the media content they desire. In New Zealand, the distribution processes assume different characteristics, since the language does not constitute a matter of concern. In addition to the organization of viewing habits that may or may not follow the official broadcasting of the TV shows, the item that is worth comparing is the attitude that fans reveal toward the different possibilities of consumption offered by the series' trans-media extensions. This analysis can help clarify (a) the current state of development of TV texts' trans-media structures, and (b) the real interest and nature of involvement that fans display in engaging with these media objects, as well as the degree of freedom that they have in exploring and shaping elements in the fictional universes.

The specificity of the media encounters between national audience groups and international fictional products refers to a convoluted set of activities that have meaningful consequences for the ways people relate to extended media content, to each other and to the world around them. In this sense, the dynamics that characterize fans' attachment toward and involvement with media products that do not belong to the culture of origin can also be investigated along the lines of "trans-cultural fandom," which recognizes that fans' affective investments in a set of characters, stories and practices move beyond national orientation and past local affiliations to where the media objects—like TV series—are produced.[5] Both *Game of Thrones* and *Mad Men* are "border-crossing" texts that—as this study shows—elicit a type of fan devotion and interpretation that display several similarities and common traits across viewing regions. This affinity of tastes and attitudes points, in Matt Hills's words, to a tendency toward "trans-cultural homology," that is, "the symbolic fit between the values and lifestyles of a group." The idea of "trans-cultural fandom" claims a perspective that transcends the specificities of the single nation, since it highlights the importance that specific processes of meaning-making, via global media encounters, have when individuals integrate media texts into their lives. Indeed, for both Italian and New Zealand fans the fictional universes of *Game of Thrones* and *Mad Men* come out as alternative realities that manage to elicit shared emotions of attraction, disgust, nostalgia and

---

[5] On the notion of transcultural fandom, see in particular, Chin and Morimoto; ; Pande.

amazement, among others. Regardless of the production country of origin (the United States) and of the countries of reception (Italy and New Zealand), these TV shows emerge as texts that are capable of reflecting on values of reference and concepts with a transcultural relevance, as well as being an effective means of virtual aggregation for their followers around the world.

Emerging practices in watching television programs can determine new ways through which the texts are produced and distributed. Binge-watching,[6] for example, is a peculiar mode of viewing television series' episodes that belongs to the age of convergence. Spectators are no longer forced to respect the programmed airing of the show; they can record the single episode, or watch it online in a streaming fashion, or illegally download it—or they can store a number of episodes (sometimes, the entire season) and watch them at a preferred time of their own choice. Viewers have turned out to be highly impatient: in the era of television "anytime, anywhere," waiting does not seem to be the best option for active consumers. Media producers have acknowledged this fact and have chosen to act accordingly: providers of on-demand streaming content such as Netflix, Amazon, Lightbox and Neon now release all episodes of a series' season in a single output, precisely to allow audiences to make their own decisions about how many episodes to watch in any one sitting. Both binge watching and the practice of illegal downloading affect media consumption at a level that is worth investigating in order to achieve a detailed picture of how people use and relate to media products today. Television is a site of convergence that unites the intimate setting of the home with the public world that extends outside the domestic area. Audience members smoothly move from one platform to the other, are capable of processing various media texts at the same time and use different spatial contexts while they are performing these multiple tasks. The inner working of this maze of procedures is dependent on factors that are specific to the country in which they occur. The close examination of national audiences' habits in assimilating media into their lives, therefore, can disclose useful data on how distinct societies develop in a world that is striving for a balance between the preservation of identities and the cultural integration at a global level.

---

[6] The expression refers to the habit of watching TV for an extended period of time like several episodes of a TV series in a row. Binge-watching has become a quite common habit among TV spectators and fans with the advent of on-demand viewing, online streaming, DVD sets and, of course, illegal downloading. Here the expression is not used in a negative sense; indeed, today it represents an important aspect of audiences' viewing habits, therefore it has to be taken into account in the analysis of these procedures.

CONCLUSIONS

A wide range of media platforms are becoming pervasive and culturally important in people's everyday lives. Screens have multiplied and have acquired new features. Some of the most important, like smaller sizes and portability, are indicative of the new consumption opportunities that are being offered to users who no longer recognize the domestic medium as the main source of information and fictional entertainment. But it is not a simple matter of technological improvement. Television texts have been changing as well in tandem with changes to the rules of the economic market, and hence the logic of monetization; they have been changing also by following paths of experimentation that have created alternative ways of approaching and experiencing media programs. The notion of "convergence culture" has helped to identify and explain these transformations on both the technological side (multiplication of media platforms, digitalization of media content) and the narrative side (trans-media storytelling). In particular, the concept of trans-media calls attention to the active role played by consumers in approaching expanded stories assembled in the guise of convoluted, fictional universes.

In the current media environment, the intertwined processes of audience fragmentation and audience autonomy (Napoli) have increased the complex nature of audience practices. Therefore, it has become more difficult to monitor and trace what it is that people are doing with and around media in their lives. Despite this, the audience as an object of study remains of key importance to understanding the significance that individuals' consumption habits have with reference to their everyday lives, especially with regard to the management of time, the impact on the various forms of personal and social interactions and the capacity of making sense of the world also as a result of the consumption of media texts.

From the reorganization of the domestic space in which laptops, tablets and mobile phones have become important viewing platforms, to the outdoors where the same devices allow their owners to enjoy personalized viewing schedules in solitude or as a social experience, audience members go through a set of daily media encounters that shape their engagement with texts and impact on the nature of their agency in consuming them. Indeed, the term "consuming" is not totally accurate to describe what people can do with the media material they come in contact with. The feeling of empowerment that audience members are experiencing today also originates from the possibility of appropriating original material in order to rework it, reedit it or repurpose it as a creative production that can, eventually, become part of the trans-media system.

The overarching purpose of this research project is to investigate the nature of national audiences' engagement with media products by asking whether their commitment to the core texts extends to the trans-media apparatus of the texts under consideration, as well as the extent to which audiences adopt, bypass or altogether ignore these alternatives. Indeed, the degree to which fans actively and imaginatively participate in these fictional universes can shed light on the mechanisms that regulate these forms of media consumption and how they are realized in specific sociocultural contexts.

This overview of audience studies, fan practices and trans-media consumption patterns informs the study in the following ways. The history of audience research demonstrates that media scholars need to be attentive to how audiences consume texts and the different meanings that they bring. Fan studies identify a particular subset of audiences who are deeply involved with media products. Such highly invested viewers feel ownership of these texts, an investment that media producers in turn want to capitalize on. Trans-media brands intensify both the opportunity for investment and for capitalization. Furthermore, studies of national audiences outside of the media texts' country of origin have shown that reception must be considered within local contexts. This project focuses on the specificities of such media practices to shed new light on the consumption patterns that distinct national audience groups adopt with reference to the same media texts. In this sense, the study will allow us to understand the popularity and the effectiveness of various trans-media extensions in different cultural contexts, and will also allow fundamental insights into the directions that audiences are moving in as active participants in transnational, trans-media contexts.

Chapter 3

NATIONAL AUDIENCES AND CONSUMPTION TRENDS IN NONDOMINANT MEDIA MARKETS

The comparative investigation of New Zealand and Italian audiences of *Game of Thrones* and *Mad Men* addresses fans' uptake of, and deviations from, a trans-media corporate strategy for the production and distribution of TV products. In doing so, this study explores the dynamics of consumers' involvement with trans-media texts as the result of their level of media literacy and engagement that is peculiar to the minor national contexts under examination. This chapter performs a statistical investigation of the main trends—in terms of viewing modes and forms of engagement—that characterize viewers' behaviors and habits.

The first phase of the data production consisted in the organization of online surveys directed at the followers of both shows in the two countries.[1] For this reason, two surveys for each show (four in total) were created with the same questions written in Italian (for the Italian audience) and in English (for the New Zealand audience). The four surveys were implemented on the website SurveyMonkey (https://www.surveymonkey.com/home/) and were, afterward, distributed on different sites. Quantitative investigations seek to establish a sufficiently large number of cases selected in such a manner as to reproduce the features of the population of interest. In this sense, questionnaires are used to outline the representative sample by requesting responses on a defined set of topics and documenting them. Statistical analysis is then performed on the responses to extract the properties of the populations under investigation in a quantitative manner. The surveys were instrumental in acquiring a general sense of audiences' behaviors and attitudes in watching and engaging with the selected TV programs and in providing a background of substantial information for the next phase of data production, the focus group sessions.

---

[1] See Appendix I: Survey Questions at the end of this thesis for a complete list of the questions used in the online surveys related to both the shows and the respondents.

In this regard, the questionnaires allowed me to investigate the different habits and perceptions espoused by participants by quantifying how often these occur and what correlations exist between them. In the chapters that follow, the qualitative analysis allows the exploration of the underlying reasons and motivations, in terms of emotional investment and negotiations of meanings, that emerged during conversational processes. These provide a key to learning and interpreting the deep dynamics of the quantitatively observed behaviors and attitudes through the freely evolving expression of feelings, preferences and interests. The results of the investigation call attention to tendencies that reveal significant correlations between (a) the cultures of origin and the ways in which the programs are watched, as well as (b) the media texts and specific forms of audience engagement. In this regard, the differences between followers of *Game of Thrones* and followers of *Mad Men* suggest that there are two "cultures of fandom," which appear to be related to the attributes that distinguish the texts' themes and storylines. The tendency of *Game of Thrones* followers is to go beyond the boundaries of the written/televisual world of the Seven Kingdoms more than the followers of Don Draper & Co. do. This essentially means that, in exceeding the viewing process, the *Game of Thrones* audiences display a higher level of investment than the *Mad Men* audience in practices that favor the exploration of the enlarged architecture of the show. The dynamics of this mode of engagement are essential to understanding the differences between distinct fan groups as well as for a proper assessment of the effectiveness of trans-media as a strategy employed by media corporations to stimulate and preserve fans' interest.

The surveys were also instrumental in finding potential participants for the qualitative phase of the data collection—the focus group sessions—that were organized in Italy and New Zealand after the launch of the questionnaires. The surveys were distributed mainly through social media pages, university websites and TV broadcasting circles. This system of advertising had the potential for selecting out specific age groups that are more prone to use such media and that are being educated at the university level. The analysis of the age group distribution shows how the correlation results depend on the age of the respondents. The possible bias effect on the conclusions by the age selection due to the choice of the advertising channels is presumably reduced by the fact that these are the same channels through which people learn news and developments about the series of interest; consequently, one would not expect the "unbiased" sample to be very much different from the one that is being targeted here. Additional investigation into the bias could be possible by using different advertisement media (newspapers, local announcements in cultural/social/institutional settings) and probing the age of respondents; however, such studies are beyond the scope of the present analysis.

The statistical tests employed to analyze the answers provided by the respondents are the chi-squared test and the *T*-test.[2] These techniques have been used to test to what degree the behavior of the respondents, in terms of viewing habits, forms of consumption and social interaction, depends on specific variables of choice. In the case of this comparative study, the findings identified by the tests allow to assess the general tendencies that characterize the respondents' behaviors and habits in relation to nationality (Italy vs. New Zealand) and program (*Game of Thrones* vs. *Mad Men*). In particular, Italians and New Zealanders display behaviors with a set of significant differences when it comes to their viewing practice and forms of engagement with the expanded structures of each TV series. These differences call attention to the fact that the culture of origin impacts on the ways international programs are watched and, in a more comprehensive sense, experienced. In addition to the nationality, the characteristics of the series under consideration (*Game of Thrones* vs. *Mad Men*) also have a role in affecting the nature of followers' involvement with the series, especially in terms of engagement in external practices that exceed the viewing activity. However, it is necessary to specify that, in this study, the number of respondents from Italy and for *Game of Thrones*, respectively, are significantly larger than the corresponding numbers for New Zealand and *Mad Men*; such differences in size of the samples constitute a limitation that translates into a high degree of uncertainty when it comes to interpretations of some data. In particular, these interpretations are to be considered more precise with regard to the followers of *Game of Thrones* than the followers of *Mad Men*.

RESPONDENT DEMOGRAPHICS—FREQUENCY TABLES

In terms of demographic composition, the following tables provide the basic information regarding the people, from Italy and New Zealand, respectively, who participated in the online surveys about *Game of Thrones* and *Mad Men*. This group of respondents will be referred to as the "sample" in this chapter. In the following tables, the "Count" indicates the number of respondents to a given question, the "Percentage" refers to the number of respondents to a given question divided by the total number of respondents to the questionnaire and the "Valid Percentage" identifies the number of respondents to a given question divided by the total number of respondents.

---

[2] The choice between the employment of the Chi-test and the *T*-test depends on the type of variable that is under consideration. That is, the Chi-test is used with *nominal* variables, whereas the *T*-test is used with *ordinal* variables.

Table 3.1 shows the total number of respondents from Italy and New Zealand, respectively, for both shows. The Italian respondents considerably outnumber the New Zealand ones, but it should also be taken into consideration that the population of Italy outnumbers that of New Zealand by approximately 13:1.

Table 3.2 classifies respondents according to the show of interest (*Game of Thrones/Mad Men*). Notably, *Game of Thrones* received a significantly higher fraction of overall responses than *Mad Men*.

Table 3.3 reports the composition of the sample in relation to gender. The numbers in the table reflect the three main genders of reference—male, female and transgender—as they were appeared in the survey question about

Table 3.1 Responses as a function of their location

	NATION		
	Count	Percentage	Valid Percentage
Italy	910	78.4	78.4
New Zealand	250	21.6	21.6
Total	1,160	100.0	100.0

Table 3.2 Responses as a function of the show of interest

	SHOW		
	Count	Percentage	Valid Percentage
Game of Thrones	965	83.2	83.2
Mad Men	195	16.8	16.8
Total	1,160	100.0	100.0

Table 3.3 Responses as a function of gender of the respondents

	GENDER		
	Count	Percentage	Valid Percentage
Male	321	27.7	33.0
Female	650	56.0	66.8
Transgender	2	0.2	0.2
Total	973	83.9	100.0
Missing[a]	187	16.1	
Total	1,160	100.0	

[a] The "Missing" value in the tables refers to the number of people who skipped the question and did not provide an answer.

Table 3.4 Responses as a function of the age of the respondents

	Count	Percentage	Valid Percentage
AGE			
19 or under	156	13.4	16.0
20–29	553	47.7	56.6
30–39	158	13.6	16.2
40–49	77	6.6	7.9
50–59	20	1.7	2.0
60–69	7	0.6	0.7
70 and over	6	0.5	0.6
Total	977	84.2	100.0
Missing	183	15.8	
Total	1,160	100.0	

gender. What emerges as relevant is that the majority of individuals who participated in the surveys identify as female, well over twice as many as identify as male.[3]

Table 3.4 reports the composition of the sample in relation to age. The numbers in the left-hand column identify eight age groups, classified according to the options that appeared in the survey question.

Table 3.4 indicates that the highest participation ratio came from respondents between the ages of 20 and 39, with a significant fall-off from age 40 and above. The majority of people who constitute the sample are, thus, between 20 and 40 years old.

Table 3.5 reports the composition of the sample in relation to level of education. The numbers in the tab identify seven groups for levels of education, classified according to the survey question about education.

In Table 3.5, the numeric values of relevance are those that refer to individuals who graduated from high school, individuals with a bachelor's degree and individuals with a bachelor (honours) degree. These data are consistent with the data from Table 3.4, which pointed out the prevalence of people under 30 responding to the surveys. Significant correlations between the variables that describe the composition of the sample, as well as these variables and the shows, are presented in the following contingency tables.

---

[3] This statement remains true even if we decide to assume that the missing number (187) of people who have chosen not to declare their gender is all males.

Table 3.5 Responses as a function of the maximum education level reached by the respondents

EDUCATION			
	Count	Percentage	Valid Percentage
Less than High School	5	0.4	0.6
Some High School, No Diploma	52	4.5	6.2
Graduated from High School	353	30.4	41.8
Bachelor's Degree	159	13.7	18.8
Bachelor (Honors) Degree	235	20.3	27.8
Master's Degrees	30	2.6	3.6
Doctorate Degree	11	0.9	1.3
Total	845	72.8	100.0
Missing	315	27.2	
Total	1,160	100.0	

SAMPLE COMPOSITION—CONTINGENCY TABLES

In statistics, a contingency table—or "crosstab"—is a table in the form of a grid that shows the frequency distribution of the variables. This provides an overview of the interrelation between two specific variables, and is instrumental in tabulating existing interactions between them. The following crosstabs present the observed correlations between the two variables of reference (NATION/SHOW)[4] and the four elements that have been taken into account as the main characteristics of the sample (gender, age, education, occupation[5]).

MAIN VARIABLE: "NATION"

In this section, the set of contingency tables focuses on the correlation between the main variable "Nation" and the other variables.

---

[4] These variables only have two values each, given that this is a comparative study between two countries (Italy and New Zealand) with two case studies (*Game of Thrones* and *Mad Men*).

[5] As for the variable "Occupation," given the preponderance of respondents under 30, it was decided to split the sample of respondents into two main categories: "Student"/ "Not Student." This is why a descriptive table of the different occupations does not appear in the previous section.

The "Nation/Gender" contingency table shows that women emerge as the dominant group both within the single nations and in a comparison between the two countries. This is to be expected given the dominance of female-identified respondents in the frequency tables.

		GENERAL			
		Male	Female	Transgender	Total
NATION					
Italy					
	Count	231	510	0	741
	Percentage in Nation	31.2%	68.8%	0.0%	100.0%
	Percentage in Gender	72.0%	78.5%	0.0%	76.2%
	Percentage of the Total	23.7%	52.4%	0.0%	76.2%
New Zealand					
	Count	90	140	2	232
	Percentage in Nation	38.8%	60.3%	0.9%	100.0%
	Percentage in Gender	28.0%	21.5%	100.0%	23.8%
	Percentage of the Total	9.2%	14.4%	0.2%	23.8%
Total					
	Count	321	650	2	973
	Percentage in Nation	33.0%	66.8%	0.2%	100.0%
	Percentage in Gender	100.0%	100.0%	100.0%	100.0%
	Percentage of the Total	33.0%	66.8%	0.2%	100.0%

The crosstab "Nation/Age" presents numeric values that identify the precise counts of the various age groups (eight groups in total, as already reported for the "Age" frequency tab) in relation to the nation from which they originate. The numbers show that the most populated groups are the first three, which identify the youngest individuals, those in age from 19 and under to 39 years. However, the age distribution of the respondents is different between Italy and New Zealand. Specifically, New Zealand features a higher fraction of respondents whose age is 19 years or less (27.8 percent vs. 12.2 percent), while the peak respondents in the age group 20–29 is relatively larger in Italy (61.6 percent vs. 40.6 percent):

		AGE GROUPS							
		19 or under	20–29	30–39	40–49	50–59	60–69	70 and over	Total
NATION									
Italy									
	Count	91	458	124	47	13	4	6	743
	Percentage in Nation	12.2%	61.6%	16.7%	6.3%	1.7%	0.5%	0.8%	100.0%
	Percentage in Age	58.3%	82.8%	78.5%	61.0%	65.0%	57.1%	100.0%	76.0%
	Percentage of the Total	9.3%	46.9%	12.7%	4.8%	1.3%	0.4%	0.6%	76.0%
New Zealand									
	Count	65	95	34	30	7	3	0	234
	Percentage in Nation	27.8%	40.6%	14.5%	12.8%	3.0%	1.3%	0.0%	100.0%
	Percentage in Age	41.7%	17.2%	21.5%	39.0%	35.0%	42.9%	0.0%	24.0%
	Percentage of the Total	6.7%	9.7%	3.5%	3.1%	0.7%	0.3%	0.0%	24.0%
Total									
	Count	156	553	158	77	20	7	6	977
	Percentage in Nation	16.0%	56.6%	16.2%	7.9%	2.0%	0.7%	0.6%	100.0%
	Percentage in Age	100%	100%	100%	100%	100%	100%	100%	100%
	Percentage of the Total	16.0%	56.6%	16.2%	7.9%	2.0%	0.7%	0.6%	100%

The "Nation/What Is Your Occupation?" crosstab presents the respondent populations as nearly evenly split between student and nonstudents, indicating that there is no prevalence of one group of viewers over the other. This appears as similar percentages for both nations:

		WHAT IS YOUR OCCUPATION?		
		Student	Nonstudent	Total
NATION				
Italy				
	Count	313	317	630
	Percentage in Nation	49.7%	50.3%	100%

WHAT IS YOUR OCCUPATION?

		Student	Nonstudent	Total
New Zealand	Percentage in What Is ...	75.1%	77.5%	76.3%
	Percentage of the Total	37.9%	38.4%	76.3%
	Count	104	92	196
	Percentage in Nation	53.1%	46.9%	100%
	Percentage in What Is...	24.9%	22.5%	23.7%
	Percentage of the Total	12.6%	11.1%	23.7%
Total	Count	417	409	826
	Percentage in Nation	50.5%	49.5%	100%
	Percentage in What Is...	100%	100%	100%
	Percentage of the Total	50.5%	49.5%	100%

MAIN VARIABLE: "SHOW"

In this section, the set of contingency tables focuses on the correlation between the main variable "Show" and the other variables.

The "Show/Gender" crosstab confirms that women are the dominant group both for *Game of Thrones* and *Mad Men*, with similar gender distributions. In this regard, it is necessary to point out that, due to the significant difference in the numbers of responses for *Game of Thrones* and *Mad Men*, the data for the former are more precise than the data for the latter. This essentially means that the data for *Game of Thrones* have a margin of uncertainty that is much lower than the data that have been collected for *Mad Men*:

		GENDER			
		Male	Female	Transgender	Total
SHOW **Game of Thrones**					
	Count	309	628	2	939
	Percentage in Show	32.9%	66.9%	0.2%	100%
	Percentage in Gender	96.3%	96.6%	100%	96.5%
	Percentage of the Total	31.8%	64.5%	0.2%	96.5%
Mad Men					
	Count	12	22	0	34
	Percentage in Show	35.3%	64.7%	0.0%	100%

		GENDER			
		Male	Female	Transgender	Total
	Percentage in Gender	3.7%	3.4%	0.0%	3.5%
	Percentage of the Total	1.2%	2.3%	0.0%	3.5%
Total					
	Count	321	650	2	973
	Percentage in Show	33%	66.8%	0.2%	100%
	Percentage in Gender	100%	100%	100%	100%
	Percentage of the Total	33%	66.8%	0.2%	100%

What emerges as significant in the "Show/Gender" contingency table is the high concentration of women as followers of *Game of Thrones*, which is generally thought to have a large resonance among men and to exert less appeal for the female portion of the audience. After all, *Game of Thrones* is filled with gruesome violence and scenes that are sexually upsetting, and the majority of these involve the submission and/or degradation of women. Our questionnaire shows, however, that the idea that *Game of Thrones* would be more "suitable" for a male audience cannot be accepted as a valid description, since, even within the limitations of this study, the female component comes out as highly significant. Were *Game of Thrones* to meet with significant disapproval among female audiences, we would see a drop in the contingency percentage compared to gender frequency, but that is not the case for this sample.

The "Show/Age" crosstab puts the shows in relation to the age of their followers. If we focus on *Game of Thrones*, it is possible to see that people under the age of 40 are by far the most numerous. The age groups 20–29 and 30–39 account for about 72 percent of the respondents, with a preponderance of those aged 20–29 (about 57 percent of the sample). The *Game of Thrones* followers account for many more responses than the *Mad Men* followers (938 vs. 39), so the distribution of age is overwhelmingly driven by the *Game of Thrones* answers.[6] The *Mad Men* followers have a distribution with much larger relative uncertainties (on the order of 30 percent), but nonetheless show that the 19-and-under group is as large as the 20–29 group within its large statistical uncertainty.

---

[6] With regard to these two crosstabs, it is worth noting the high degree of missing gender and age data for the *Mad Men* show. This indicates that *Mad Men* respondents were reluctant to provide information about their gender and age, perhaps because it was considered by these survey participants to be too personal. In particular, the information about age represents data that people might want to keep to themselves, and if we assume a

		AGE GROUPS						
		19 or under	20–29	30–39	40–49	50–59	60–69	70 and above	Total
SHOW									
Game of Thrones									
	Count	146	540	151	71	17	7	6	938
	Percentage in Show	15.6%	57.6%	16.1%	7.6%	1.8%	0.7%	0.6%	100%
	Percentage in Age	93.6%	97.6%	95.6%	92.2%	85%	100%	100%	96%
	Percentage of the Total	14.9%	55.3%	15.5%	7.3%	1.7%	0.7%	0.6%	96%
Mad Men									
	Count	10	13	7	6	3	0	0	39
	Percentage in Show	25.6%	33.3%	17.9%	15.4%	7.7%	0%	0%	100%
	Percentage in Age	6.4%	2.4%	4.4%	7.8%	15%	0%	0%	4%
	Percentage of the Total	1%	1.3%	0.7%	0.6%	0.3%	0%	0%	4%
Total									
	Count	156	553	158	77	20	7	6	977
	Percentage in Show	16%	56.6%	16.2%	7.9%	2%	0.7%	0.6%	100%
	Percentage in Age	100%	100%	100%	100%	100%	100%	100%	100%
	Percentage of the Total	16%	56.6%	16.2%	7.9%	2%	0.7%	0.6%	100%

In the "Show/Education" crosstab, the "Graduated from High School" group and the "Bachelor's (Honors) Degree" groups dominate the sample, with the former being the most populous for *Game of Thrones*. The *Mad Men* followers' distribution is different, as it peaks on the "Bachelor's (Honors) Degree" sample (38.3 percent of the total), with "Graduated from High School" sample being the second largest, albeit all with larger uncertainties than *Game of Thrones* given the reduced sample size.

---

greater number of older individuals among the *Mad Men* respondents than among the *Game of Thrones* ones, this could explain the significant amount of missing data for the former series.

EDUCATION

	Less than High School	Some High School, No Diploma	Graduated from High School	Bachelor's Degree	Bachelor (Honors) Degree	Master's Degree	Doctorate Degree	Total
SHOW								
Game of Thrones								
Count	5	46	314	137	189	24	10	725
Percentage in Show	0.7%	6.3%	43.3%	18.9%	26.1%	3.3%	1.4%	100%
Percentage in Education	100%	88.5%	89%	86.2%	80.4%	80%	90.9%	85.8%
Percentage of the Total	0.6%	5.4%	37.2%	16.2%	22.4%	2.8%	1.2%	85.8%
Mad Men								
Count	0	6	39	22	46	6	1	120
Percentage in Show	0%	5%	32.5%	18.3%	38.3%	5%	0.8%	100%
Percentage in Education	0%	11.5%	11%	13.8%	19.6%	20%	9.1%	14.2%
Percentage of the Total	0%	0.7%	4.6%	2.6%	5.4%	0.7%	0.1%	14.2%
Total								
Count	5	52	353	159	235	30	11	845
Percentage in Show	0.6%	6.2%	41.8%	18.8%	27.8%	3.6%	1.3%	100%
Percentage in Education	100%	100%	100%	100%	100%	100%	100%	100%
Percentage of the Total	0.6%	6.2%	41.8%	18.8%	27.8%	3.6%	1.3%	100%

The "Show/What is your occupation?" contingency table shows that the set of followers tends to be nearly evenly split between students and nonstudents as a function of the show. For *Game of Thrones*, student and non-student populations are nearly the same size; for *Mad Men*, the population of nonstudents is slightly larger than student viewers. However, given the smaller sample size compared to the *Game of Thrones* sample, the values are actually consistent (52 ± 7 is consistent with 63 ± 8) and more data would be needed to confirm such a trend:

		Student	Nonstudent	Total
		WHAT IS YOUR OCCUPATION?		
SHOW				
Game of Thrones				
	Count	365	346	711
	Percentage in Show	51.3%	48.7%	100%
	Percentage in What Is	87.5%	84.6%	86.1%
	...			
	Percentage of the Total	44.2%	41.9%	86.1%
Mad Men				
	Count	52	63	115
	Percentage in Show	45.2%	54.8%	100%
	Percentage in What Is	12.5%	15.4%	13.9%
	...			
	Percentage of the Total	6.3%	7.6%	13.9%
Total				
	Count	417	409	826
	Percentage in Show	50.5%	49.5%	100%
	Percentage in What Is...	100%	100%	100%
	Percentage of the Total	50.5%	49.5%	100%

CHI-SQUARED (χ^2) TEST—DEFINITION

The χ^2 test[7] provides the measure of the significance of the discrepancy between the observed data and the prediction provided by a given model.[8]

---

[7] The chi-squared test is used to test whether the behavior of Italians and New Zealanders is consistent independently of a certain feature of the respondents by analyzing the values in 2 × 2 contingency tables. For a comprehensive description of the chi-squared test and its properties and functions, see Field (2013).

[8] If the model describes the data and the number of counts is large (generally above 30), the probability distribution for the values of this X^2 is known to be a χ^2 with N degrees

In the present analysis, the χ^2 test offers a model of compared responses to specific questions regarding the observed data in many two-way (2 × 2) contingency tables used to correlate one property X to another property Y. The model assumes that the probability of making certain observations about X is independent of Y. In the case of this study, the model that generates the predictions assumes that the counts observed as answers to a given question are independent of what nation the respondents belong to, or of what show the respondents are answering about. This means that the model assumes that the distribution of the percentages of the answers to a given question will be the same in Italy and in New Zealand or the same for *Game of Thrones* and *Mad Men*. The chi-squared test is instrumental in pointing out a dependence ("significant association") between the nationality (Italy vs. New Zealand) or the show (*Game of Thrones* vs. *Mad Men*) and the modes of consumption which the respondents engage in. This dependence calls attention to the fact that specific behaviors emerge as different rather than identical when Italy and New Zealand are compared (which means that there is a correlation between the nations and the investigated behaviors) or when *Game of Thrones* and *Mad Men* are compared (which means that there is a correlation between the shows and the investigated behaviors).

All the tables reported below are 2 × 2 contingency tables that show the correlations between the indicated variables (with the main variables "Nation" and "Show" as the constant ones) for the two options "Yes" and "No." The "Yes" and "No" options have been applied to each question with the final goal of running the chi-squared test, since it is necessary to have two response modes in order to create a single contingency table. In addition to the counts, all the tables report the fraction that each count represents as a function of (a) the number of respondents totalling both "Yes" and "No" values; (b) the total number of respondents along the column (within a given nation) and (c) the total number of respondents along the row (within the "Yes" class or within the "No" class).

---

of freedom, where N is the number of measurements minus (1 + number of parameters that are determined by the test). The hypothesis that the model describes the observation is called "null hypothesis." The probability to obtain a value of χ^2 that is more discrepant than the one observed in the data is calculable and if such probability is smaller than a given predetermined threshold (significance value) the "null" hypothesis is rejected. The formula to calculate the χ^2 function uses the pairs of observed and predicted counts in a given class and it is built as follows:

$$\sum_{1}^{NClass} \mathrm{class} \frac{(v(\mathrm{class})_{observed} - v(\mathrm{class})_{predicted})^2}{v(\mathrm{class})_{predicted}}$$

On this topic, see Snedecor and Cochran (1989).

See also: http://www.itl.nist.gov/div898/handbook/eda/section4/eda43.htm#Snedecor (accessed November 10, 2017).

CHI-SQUARED TEST RESULTS—SIGNIFICANT ASSOCIATIONS FOR THE MAIN VARIABLE "NATION"

With reference to the question from the online survey that asked about the preferred modality for watching the series' episodes,[9] the chi-squared test indicates a significant difference between the two countries in the employment of devices like DVR or TiVo for recording the series' episodes.

DVR/TiVo

YES	Italy	New Zealand	Total	NO	Italy	New Zealand	Total
Count	100	13	113	Count	810	237	1,047
Expected Count	88.6	24.4	113	Expected Count	821.4	225.6	1,047.0
Percentage in DVR/TiVo	88.5%	11.5%	100%	Percentage in DVR/TiVo	77.4%	22.6%	100%
Percentage in Nation	11.0%	5.2%	9.7%	Percentage in Nation	89.0%	94.8%	90.3%
Percentage of the total	8.6%	1.1%	9.7%	Percentage of the total	69.8%	20.4%	90.3%

The corresponding values of the χ^2 for each of the reported tables can be found in Appendix II: χ^2 Values.

In particular, even though the respondents who record the series are a minority in both Italy and New Zealand, their fraction is significantly higher in Italy (11 percent) than in New Zealand (5 percent).

With reference to the time of viewing for watching the shows,[10] the chi-squared test reveals a significant association between the variable "Nation" and each of the four options listed ("In the Morning," "In the Afternoon," "In the Evening," "During the Night"), with a main trend pointing in the

---

[9] *If you do not watch the episodes live, how do you watch them?*
    On DVR/TiVo
    On DVDs
    On iTunes
    Through legal streaming services
    Other
[10] *What time do you usually prefer watching the show's episodes?*
    In the morning (6 a.m.–12 p.m.)
    In the afternoon (12 p.m.–6.p.m.)
    In the evening (6 p.m.–11 p.m.)
    During the night (11 p.m.–6 a.m.)

direction of the third option—"In the Evening"—as the preferred timeframe for watching the TV programs:

In the Morning

YES	Italy	New Zealand	Total	NO	Italy	New Zealand	Total
Count	32	0	32	Count	878	250	1,128
Expected Count	25.1	6.9	32.0	Expected Count	884.9	243.1	1,128.0
Percentage in "In the Morning"	100.0%	0.0%	100.0%	Percentage in "In the Morning"	77.8%	22.2%	100.0%
Percentage in Nation	3.5%	0.0%	2.8%	Percentage in Nation	96.5%	100.0%	97.2%
Percentage of the Total	2.8%	0.0%	2.8%	Percentage of the Total	75.7%	21.6%	97.2%

In the Afternoon

YES	Italy	New Zealand	Total	NO	Italy	New Zealand	Total
Count	126	16	142	Count	784	234	1,018
Expected Count	111.4	30.6	142.0	Expected Count	798.6	219.4	1,018.0
Percentage in "In the afternoon"	88.7%	11.3%	100.0%	Percentage in "In the Afternoon"	77.0%	23.0%	100.0%
Percentage in Nation	13.8%	6.4%	12.2%	Percentage in Nation	86.2%	93.6%	87.8%
Percentage of the total	10.9%	1.4%	12.2%	Percentage of the total	67.6%	20.2%	87.8%

In the Evening

YES	Italy	New Zealand	Total	NO	Italy	New Zealand	Total
Count	487	219	706	Count	423	31	454
Expected Count	553.8	152.2	706.0	Expected Count	356.2	97.8	454.0
Percentage in "In the evening"	69.0%	31.0%	100.0%	Percentage in "In the evening"	93.2%	6.8%	100.0%

In the Evening

YES	Italy	New Zealand	Total	NO	Italy	New Zealand	Total
Percentage in Nation	53.5%	87.6%	60.9%	Percentage in Nation	46.5%	12.4%	39.1%
Percentage of the Total	42.0%	18.9%	60.9%	Percentage of the Total	36.5%	2.7%	39.1%

During the Night

YES	Italy	New Zealand	Total	NO	Italy	New Zealand	Total
Count	106	9	115	Count	804	241	1,045
Expected Count	90.2	24.8	115.0	Expected Count	819.8	225.2	1,045.0
Percentage in "During the Night"	92.2%	7.8%	100.0%	Percentage in "During the Night"	76.9%	23.1%	100.0%
Percentage in Nation	11.6%	3.6%	9.9%	Percentage in Nation	88.4%	96.4%	90.1%
Percentage of the Total	9.1%	0.8%	9.9%	Percentage of the Total	69.3%	20.8%	90.1%

In the case of the morning, the majority of the sample (97.2 percent) does not opt for this timeframe for watching the show. Within this main trend, only 3.5 percent of the Italian sample takes advantage of this period, whereas the New Zealand sample appears not to take this timeframe into consideration at all (no respondent from New Zealand chose this option). In the case of the afternoon, the general tendency (87.8 percent of the sample) is to not watch the shows during this part of the day. Nevertheless, 13.8 percent of the Italian sample and 6.8 percent of the New Zealand sample refer to this timeframe for the viewing. This means that Italian viewers take advantage of this timeframe for watching the programs more than New Zealanders do. In the case of the evening, the majority of viewers from both countries (60.9 percent of the total sample) prefer this part of the day for watching the series. In particular, within this main trend, New Zealand viewers (87.6 percent) have a particular predilection for the evening as the best time for watching the series in comparison to the Italian ones (53.5 percent). In the case of the night, 90.1 percent of the total sample chooses not to watch the programs during this timeframe. The fraction of New Zealand viewers who do not watch the show at night, however, is more dominant than the Italian one.

When it comes to the practice of engaging in parallel activities during the viewing time,[11] the chi-squared test points out a differential trend between Italy and New Zealand identified by the option: "I do not do anything else while watching the show":

I do not do anything else while watching the show							
YES	Italy	New Zealand	Total	NO	Italy	New Zealand	Total
Count	674	120	794	Count	236	130	366
Expected Count	622.9	171.1	794.0	Expected Count	287.1	78.9	366.0
Percentage in "I do not do anything else …"	84.9%	15.1%	100.0%	Percentage in "I do not do anything else …"	64.5%	35.5%	100.0%
Percentage in Nation	74.1%	48.0%	68.4%	Percentage in Nation	25.9%	52.0%	31.6%
Percentage of the Total	58.1%	10.3%	68.4%	Percentage of the Total	20.3%	11.2%	31.6%

In particular, the tendency for the Italian sample is to not engage in parallel activities while watching the shows (~74 percent of respondents do nothing when watching the show), whereas New Zealand viewers tend to be split nearly equally between those who do nothing else while watching the show (48 percent) and those who are also engaged in other activities (52 percent). This is a potentially significant difference, given that expanded viewing practices in general, and trans-media engagement more specifically, often takes place as parallel activities to watching a program (e.g., second-screening activities). If the Italian sample shows a considerably lower likelihood of engaging in parallel activities than the New Zealand sample, this may align with a lower likelihood of pursuing concurrent trans-media options.

---

[11] **When you watch the show, is it usually the only thing you are doing? (Tick all that apply)**
   I do not do anything else while watching the show
   I engage in domestic tasks (cooking, cleaning, etc.)
   I chat with people offline and/or online
   I chat with people offline and/or online about the episode I am watching
   I surf the net
   I play games
   Other

As for the practice of interacting with others during the viewing time,[12] the chi-squared test highlights the existence of distinct behaviors between Italians and New Zealanders in relation to the two options: "No, I watch the episodes by myself" and "Yes, I post comments on the official Facebook/Twitter pages of the series about the episode I am watching."

No, I watch the episodes by myself

YES	Italy	New Zealand	Total	NO	Italy	New Zealand	Total
Count	532	108	640	Count	378	142	520
Expected Count	502.1	137.9	640.0	Expected Count	407.9	112.1	520.0
Percentage in "No, I Watch the Episodes by Myself"	83.1%	16.9%	100.0%	Percentage in "No, I Watch the Episodes by Myself"	72.7%	27.3%	100.0%
Percentage in Nation	58.5%	43.2%	55.2%	Percentage in Nation	41.5%	56.8%	44.8%
Percentage of the Total	45.9%	9.3%	55.2%	Percentage of the Total	32.6%	12.2%	44.8%

Yes, I post comments on the official Facebook/Twitter pages of the series about the episode I am watching

YES	Italy	New Zealand	Total	NO	Italy	New Zealand	Total
Count	30	0	30	Count	880	250	1,130
Expected Count	23.5	6.5	30.0	Expected Count	886.5	243.5	1,130.0
Percentage in "Yes, I Post Comments…"	100.0%	0.0%	100.0%	Percentage in "Yes, I Post Comments…"	77.9%	22.1%	100.0%

[12] **When you watch the show, are you usually engaging with others? (Tick all that apply)**

No, I watch the episodes by myself
Yes, I watch the episodes with my family at home
Yes, I watch the episodes with my friends at my house
Yes, I watch the episodes with my friends at someone else's house
Yes, I watch with my family/friends who are somewhere else through synchronous viewing on one or more technological devices
Yes, I post comments on the official Facebook/Twitter pages of the series about the episode I am watching

Yes, I post comments on the official Facebook/Twitter pages of the series about the episode I am watching

YES	Italy	New Zealand	Total	NO	Italy	New Zealand	Total
Percentage in Nation	3.3%	0.0%	2.6%	Percentage in Nation	96.7%	100.0%	97.4%
Percentage of the Total	2.6%	0.0%	2.6%	Percentage of the Total	75.9%	21.6%	97.4%

In the case of the first option, Italian viewers (58.5 percent in the "Yes" category) display a more significant tendency to watch the programs by themselves in comparison to New Zealanders (56.8 percent in the "No" category). As for the second option, the dominant trend for both nationalities goes counter to posting comments during the viewing process. However, within this negative tendency, the percentage for the New Zealand sample (100 percent) is higher than the percentage for the Italian sample (96.7 percent), indicating that New Zealanders refuse all engagement with such posts while watching the shows.

With reference to the activity of producing original media material related to the series,[13] the chi-squared test signals a relevant association between the variable "Nation" and the option "Photo collages/Posters." Nonetheless, the main tendency for both groups (92.6 percent of the total sample) is to not engage in this production practice.

Photo collages/Posters

YES	Italy	New Zealand	Total	NO	Italy	New Zealand	Total
Count	82	4	86	Count	828	246	1,074
Expected Count	67.5	18.5	86.0	Expected Count	842.5	231.5	1,074.0
Percentage in "Photo Collages/ Posters"	95.3%	4.7%	100.0%	Percentage in "Photo Collages/ Posters"	77.1%	22.9%	100.0%
Percentage in Nation	9.0%	1.6%	7.4%	Percentage in Nation	91.0%	98.4%	92.6%

---

[13] ***Do you produce media content related to the series? Choose from the list:***
Mash-ups
Music videos

Photo collages/Posters

YES	Italy	New Zealand	Total	NO	Italy	New Zealand	Total
Percentage of the Total	7.1%	0.3%	7.4%	Percentage of the Total	71.4%	21.2%	92.6%

The negative tendency is more significant in the case of New Zealand (only 1.6 percent of the respondents produce photo and collages) than in the case of Italy (about 9 percent of the respondents engage in photo/poster production), suggesting that Italian viewers to some small degree create photo collages or posters.

With reference to the practice of taking part in social media activities regarding the shows,[14] the chi-squared test reveals a significant association between the variable "Nation" and the three options: "No, I do not," "Yes, I follow them but I do not post anything" and "Yes, I follow them and I also post comments."

No, I do not

YES	Italy	New Zealand	Total	NO	Italy	New Zealand	Total
Count	127	154	281	Count	783	96	879
Expected Count	220.4	60.6	281.0	Expected Count	689.6	189.4	879.0
Percentage in "No, I Do Not"	45.2%	54.8%	100.0%	Percentage in "No, I Do Not"	89.1%	10.9%	100.0%
Percentage in Nation	14.0%	61.6%	24.2%	Percentage in Nation	86.0%	38.4%	75.8%
Percentage of the Total	10.9%	13.3%	24.2%	Percentage of the Total	67.5%	8.3%	75.8%

Clips
Web-based animations
Photo collages/Posters
Other (please specify)

[14] **Do you follow the updates and/or post comments on the official Facebook/Twitter pages of the series?**
No, I do not
Yes, I follow them but I do not post anything
Yes, I follow them and I also post comments

Yes, I follow them but I do not post anything

YES	Italy	New Zealand	Total	NO	Italy	New Zealand	Total
Count	464	74	538	Count	446	176	622
Expected Count	422.1	115.9	538.0	Expected Count	487.9	134.1	622.0
Percentage in "Yes, I Follow Them but I Do Not Post Anything"	86.2%	13.8%	100.0%	Percentage in "Yes, I Follow Them but I Do Not Post Anything"	71.7%	28.3%	100.0%
Percentage in Nation	51.0%	29.6%	46.4%	Percentage in Nation	49.0%	70.4%	53.6%
Percentage of the Total	40.0%	6.4%	46.4%	Percentage of the Total	38.4%	15.2%	53.6%

Yes, I follow them and I also post comments

YES	Italy	New Zealand	Total	NO	Italy	New Zealand	Total
Count	165	4	169	Count	745	246	991
Expected Count	132.6	36.4	169.0	Expected Count	777.4	213.6	991.0
Percentage in "Yes, I Follow Them and I Also Post Comments"	97.6%	2.4%	100.0%	Percentage in "Yes, I Follow Them and I Also Post Comments"	75.2%	24.8%	100.0%
Percentage in Nation	18.1%	1.6%	14.6%	Percentage in Nation	81.9%	98.4%	85.4%
Percentage of the Total	14.2%	0.3%	14.6%	Percentage of the Total	64.2%	21.2%	85.4%

Comparatively, the Italian respondents overwhelmingly favor following updates (only 14 percent of them chose the "No, I do not" option), while New Zealand viewers are predominantly in favor of not following updates (a majority of ~62 percent of respondents supports the "No, I do not" option). The dominant trend for the Italian sample (51.0 percent in the "Yes" category) is to follow the updates without posting, whereas the majority of the New Zealand sample does not display the same interest in this practice (70.4 percent in the "No" category). As for following and posting, the general tendency for both nationalities goes in the direction of the "No," with a more significant negative percentage represented by the New Zealand sample (98.4 percent).

CHI-SQUARED TEST RESULTS—SIGNIFICANT ASSOCIATIONS FOR THE MAIN VARIABLE "SHOW"

With reference to the question from the online survey that asked about the overall number of episodes that have been watched,[15] the dominant tendency goes in the direction of being up to date with the viewing of the series.

Numbers of episodes watched

YES	Game of Thrones	Mad Men	Total	NO	Game of Thrones	Mad Men	Total
Count	817	135	952	Count	148	60	208
Expected Count	792.0	160.0	952.0	Expected Count	173.0	35.0	208.0
Percentage in "Have You Watched All the Episodes ..."	85.8%	14.2%	100.0%	Percentage in "Have You Watched All the Episodes ..."	71.2%	28.8%	100.0%
Percentage in Show	84.7%	69.2%	82.1%	Percentage in Show	15.3%	30.8%	17.9%
Percentage of the Total	70.4%	11.6%	82.1%	Percentage of the Total	12.8%	5.2%	17.9%

The corresponding values of the χ^2 for each of the reported tables can be found in Appendix II: χ^2 Values.

In particular, this trend emerges as more significant for *Game of Thrones* (~85 percent) than *Mad Men* (~69 percent). This fact can be explained with regard to the textual attributes that characterize the two series. *Game of Thrones'* storylines are filled with more twists and turns than *Mad Men*, whose narrative is less centered around the construction of suspense. Consequently, when it comes to *Game of Thrones*, in order to properly understand and follow the complex developments of the plot, viewer practice reflects a need to stay up to date with the episodes in a season.

---

[15] *Have you watched all the episodes of the seasons of the show so far?*
   Yes
   No

As for the preferred time of viewing,[16] the chi-squared test reveals a significant association with regard to the two options of the evening and the night.

In the Evening

YES	Game of Thrones	Mad Men	Total	NO	Game of Thrones	Mad Men	Total
Count	610	96	706	Count	355	99	454
Expected Count	587.3	118.7	706.0	Expected Count	377.7	76.3	454.0
Percentage in "In the Evening"	86.4%	13.6%	100.0%	Percentage in "In the Evening"	78.2%	21.8%	100.0%
Percentage in Show	63.2%	49.2%	60.9%	Percentage in Show	36.8%	50.8%	39.1%
Percentage of the Total	52.6%	8.3%	60.9%	Percentage of the Total	30.6%	8.5%	39.1%

During the Night

YES	Game of Thrones	Mad Men	Total	NO	Game of Thrones	Mad Men	Total
Count	88	27	115	Count	877	168	1,045
Expected Count	95.7	19.3	115.0	Expected Count	869.3	175.7	1,045.0
Percentage in "During the Night"	76.5%	23.5%	100.0%	Percentage in "During the Night"	83.9%	16.1%	100.0%
Percentage in Show	9.1%	13.8%	9.9%	Percentage in Show	90.9%	86.2%	90.1%
Percentage of the Total	7.6%	2.3%	9.9%	Percentage of the Total	75.6%	14.5%	90.1%

---

[16] ***What time do you usually prefer watching the show's episodes?***
  In the morning (6 a.m.–12 p.m.)
  In the afternoon (12 p.m.–6 p.m.)
  In the evening (6 p.m.–11 p.m.)
  During the night (11 p.m.–6 a.m.)

The evening emerges as the timeframe of preference for watching *Game of Thrones* (86.4 percent of the sample in the "Yes" category), while in the case of *Mad Men* the respondents are evenly split between those who watch the show in the evening (~49 percent) and those who don't (~51 percent). As for the night, the dominant trend for both shows is not to watch during this timeframe, with a general tendency toward the "No" that is more significant for *Game of Thrones* (~91 percent) than for *Mad Men* (~86 percent). The evening turns out to be the preferred timeframe for all viewing activities, in particular with regard to the TV series *Game of Thrones*.

With regard to performing parallel tasks during the time of viewing,[17] the chi-squared test signals a relevant association with regard to the two options: "I chat with people offline and/or online" and "I chat with people offline and/or online about the episode I am watching":

I chat with people offline and/or online

YES	Game of Thrones	Mad Men	Total	NO	Game of Thrones	Mad Men	Total
Count	49	2	51	Count	916	193	1,109
Expected Count	42.4	8.6	51.0	Expected Count	922.6	186.4	1,109.0
Percentage in "I Chat with People Offline and/or Online"	96.1%	3.9%	100.0%	Percentage in "I Chat with People Offline and/or Online"	82.6%	17.4%	100.0%
Percentage in Show	5.1%	1.0%	4.4%	Percentage in Show	94.9%	99.0%	95.6%
Percentage of the Total	4.2%	0.2%	4.4%	Percentage of the Total	79.0%	16.6%	95.6%

[17] **When you watch the show, is it usually the only thing you are doing? (Tick all that apply)**
> *I do not do anything else while watching the show*
> *I engage in domestic tasks (cooking, cleaning, etc.)*
> *I chat with people offline and/or online*
> *I chat with people offline and/or online about the episode I am watching*
> *I surf the net*
> *I play games*
> *Other*

I chat with people offline and/or online about the episode I am watching

YES	Game of Thrones	Mad Men	Total	NO	Game of Thrones	Mad Men	Total
Count	55	1	56	Count	910	194	1,104
Expected Count	46.6	9.4	56.0	Expected Count	918.4	185.6	1,104.0
Percentage in "I Chat with People Offline and/or Online…"	98.2%	1.8%	100.0%	Percentage in "I Chat with People Offline and/or Online…"	82.4%	17.6%	100.0%
Percentage in Show	5.7%	0.5%	4.8%	Percentage in Show	94.3%	99.5%	95.2%
Percentage of the Total	4.7%	0.1%	4.8%	Percentage of the Total	78.4%	16.7%	95.2%

The dominant tendency, for both series, is to not engage in this type of activities during the time of viewing, but within the dominant trend the orientation toward "No" is more significant in the case of *Mad Men* (~99 percent) than in the case of *Game of Thrones* (~95 percent).

With reference to the practice of interacting with others during the time of viewing,[18] the chi-squared test points out a significant association with regard to the option: "No, I watch the episodes by myself."

No, I watch the episodes by myself

YES	Game of Thrones	Mad Men	Total	NO	Game of Thrones	Mad Men	Total
Count	514	126	640	Count	451	69	520
Expected Count	532.4	107.6	640.0	Expected Count	432.6	87.4	520.0
Percentage in "No, I Watch the Episodes by Myself"	80.3%	19.7%	100.0%	Percentage in "No, I Watch the Episodes by Myself"	86.7%	13.3%	100.0%
Percentage in Show	53.3%	64.6%	55.2%	Percentage in Show	46.7%	35.4%	44.8%
Percentage of the Total	44.3%	10.9%	55.2%	Percentage of the Total	38.9%	5.9%	44.8%

---

[18] ***When you watch the show, are you usually engaging with others? (Tick all that apply)***
   No, I watch the episodes by myself

Viewers of both programs tend to watch the episodes alone (55.2 percent of the total in the "Yes" category), but within this general trend this activity emerges as more relevant for *Mad Men* (64.6 percent) than *Game of Thrones* (53.3 percent).

As for the question from the online survey that asked about social media–related activities,[19] the chi-squared test reveals that fans of the two shows have different behaviors in relation to the practices associated with posting comments.

No, I do not

YES	Game of Thrones	Mad Men	Total	NO	Game of Thrones	Mad Men	Total
Count	252	29	281	Count	713	166	879
Expected Count	233.8	47.2	281.0	Expected Count	731.2	147.8	879.0
Percentage in "No, I Do Not"	89.7%	10.3%	100.0%	Percentage in "No, I Do Not"	81.1%	18.9%	100.0%
Percentage in Show	26.1%	14.9%	24.2%	Percentage in Show	73.9%	85.1%	75.8%
Percentage of the Total	21.7%	2.5%	24.2%	Percentage of the Total	61.5%	14.3%	75.8%

Yes, I watch the episodes with my family at home

Yes, I watch the episodes with my friends at my house

Yes, I watch the episodes with my friends at someone else's house

Yes, I watch with my family/friends who are somewhere else through synchronous viewing on one or more technological devices

Yes, I post comments on the official Facebook/Twitter pages of the series about the episode I am watching

[19] **Do you follow the updates and/or post comments on the official Facebook/Twitter pages of the series?**

No, I do not

Yes, I follow them but I do not post anything

Yes, I follow them and I also post comments

Yes, I follow them but I do not post anything

YES	Game of Thrones	Mad Men	Total	NO	Game of Thrones	Mad Men	Total
Count	529	9	538	Count	436	186	622
Expected Count	447.6	90.4	538.0	Expected Count	517.4	104.6	622.0
Percentage in "Yes, I Follow Them but …"	98.3%	1.7%	100.0%	Percentage in "Yes, I Follow Them but …"	70.1%	29.9%	100.0%
Percentage in Show	54.8%	4.6%	46.4%	Percentage in Show	45.2%	95.4%	53.6%
Percentage of the Total	45.6%	0.8%	46.4%	Percentage of the Total	37.6%	16.0%	53.6%

Yes, I follow them and I also post comments

YES	Game of Thrones	Mad Men	Total	NO	Game of Thrones	Mad Men	Total
Count	163	6	169	Count	802	189	991
Expected Count	140.6	28.4	169.0	Expected Count	824.4	166.6	991.0
Percentage in "No, I Do Not"	96.4%	3.6%	100.0%	Percentage in "No, I Do Not"	80.9%	19.1%	100.0%
Percentage in Show	16.9%	3.1%	14.6%	Percentage in Show	83.1%	96.9%	85.4%
Percentage of the Total	14.1%	0.5%	14.6%	Percentage of the Total	69.1%	16.3%	85.4%

In particular, a positive response emerges as relevant for *Game of Thrones* (~55 percent of respondents supports following without posting), whereas for *Mad Men* it goes overwhelmingly in the opposite direction (only ~5 percent of respondents favors following without posting). This means that, when it comes to *Game of Thrones* in comparison to *Mad Men*, viewers display a significant tendency toward following the online posts and updates related to the former. Indeed, in the case of *Game of Thrones* the main tendency is to follow the updates and the comments on social media without necessarily participating in the conversation, whereas when it comes to *Mad Men* not even the practice of following updates emerges as notably relevant.

T-TEST—DEFINITION

The *T*-test[20] is a method of testing hypotheses about the mean of a small sample chosen from a set of events that is presumed normally distributed. It is usually employed to test the hypothesis that the observed mean of a small sample is consistent with the mean of the assumed population model.[21] In the present analysis, the *T*-test is used to compare the mean behavior of the respondents from New Zealand and Italy with respect to certain questions, and to check whether they are significantly different from each other. The *T*-test takes a different mathematical form depending on whether the spread of the choices around the average is considered to be the same in Italy and New Zealand. This information is initially determined by performing another statistical test called Levene's test.[22] Similarly to the χ^2 test, a critical value for a variable built from the data is determined from the expected distribution of the responses: this is obtained by assuming that New Zealand and Italy have either the same spread around the average (for the Levene's test) or the same average

---

[20] The *T*-test is used to investigate questions implying discrepancies between average behaviors of Italians and New Zealanders. The *T*-test is employed because it checks the consistency of the average between two Gaussian distributions.

For a comprehensive description of the *T*-test and its properties and functions, see Field (2013).

[21] Given the observed values of the sample, a test statistic called *T* is defined as:

$$\frac{x - \mu}{s/\sqrt{n}}$$

where x is the mean value of the sample, μ is the assumed population mean, s is the estimate of the standard deviation of the sample and n is the sample size. In the assumption of this "null hypothesis," the test-statistic T is distributed as a Student's t-distribution with $n-1$ degrees of freedom, where the number of degrees of freedom is given by the number of events in the sample. In the present analysis the test is specialized to compare the means of two distributions of counts, that is, to test whether the hypothesis that the two means from two independent samples, assumed to follow the same distribution, are the same. The mean of a distribution of respondents to a given reply is defined by assigning an integer value to each class of respondents according to the order their class has in the list of replies and by summing the value of each respondent class weighted by the fraction of the total respondents in the class, that is,

$\mu = \sum_{k=0}^{N} k f_k$ where k is the integer position of class k and $f_k = \frac{N_k}{N}$ is the ratio of N_k, the number of respondents in class k, to N, the total number of respondents.

On this topic, see Snedecor and Cochran (1989).

See also: "Confidence Limits for the Mean," http://www.itl.nist.gov/div898/handbook/eda/section3/eda352.htm (accessed November 10, 2017).

[22] See *Levene (278–92)*.

(for the *T*-test) and by requiring that the probability of observing a larger value than the critical value is smaller than 5 percent. If the observed value is larger than the critical value, the assumption that the average for the responses are equal between Italy and New Zealand must be rejected, and the average for the values of the responses is therefore considered significantly different.

T-TEST RESULTS FOR THE MAIN VARIABLE "NATION"

The following trends are the significant differences between Italians and New Zealanders highlighted by the *T*-test results with regard to the main variable "Nation."

With reference to how the episodes are watched (live or not)[23] and the preferred platforms for the viewing,[24] the *T*-test results indicate that, on average, New Zealanders employ the computer and engage in the practice of binge-watching[25] more than the Italians. The latter, by contrast, tend to watch the

---

[23] **Do you watch the show's episodes live on television?**
   Never
   Rarely
   Sometimes
   Often
   Always
   Italy ($M = 2.04$); New Zealand ($M = 1.57$); ("M" stands for "Mean," that indicates the average of a set of data).

[24] **On which platform(s) do you tend to watch the show more often?**

	Never	Rarely	Sometimes	Often	Always
Television					
Computer					
Tablet					
Mobile Phone					
Screens in Public Spaces					
Other					

The corresponding values of M for the "Computer," "Tablet" and the "Mobile Phone" options are, respectively:
   New Zealanders ($M = 3.91$); Italy ($M = 3.68$);
   Italy ($M = 1.78$); (New Zealand ($M = 1.45$);
   Italy ($M = 1.43$); New Zealand ($M = 1.29$).

[25] **Do you watch three or more episodes of the series in a single sitting?**
   Never
   Rarely
   Sometimes
   Often
   Always
   New Zealand ($M = 2.95$); Italy ($M = 2.71$).

programs live and to use the tablet and the mobile phone for the same activity more than New Zealanders do.

Episodes Watched Live

Levene's Test	Significance	T	Degrees of Freedom	Significance (Two-Tailed)
42.786	0.000	5.514	509.999	0.000

Platforms

	Levene's Test	Significance	T	Degrees of Freedom	Significance (Two-Tailed)
Computer	24.814	0.000	−2.210	388.663	0.028
Tablet	31.091	0.000	3.754	296.704	0.000
Mobile Phone	10.3888	0.001	1.987	276.855	0.048

Binge-Watching

Levene's Test	Significance	T	Degrees of Freedom	Significance (Two-Tailed)
12.490	0.000	−3.285	414.559	0.001

With reference to the general trend of visiting the official websites of the series,[26] as well as alternative websites about the programs,[27] the T-test results point out that, on average, Italians are more active than New Zealanders in this regard. Italians also tend to take part in

---

[26] ***Do you visit the show's official website?***
Never
Rarely
Sometimes
Often
Always
Italy ($M = 2.14$); New Zealand ($M = 1.48$).

[27] ***Do you visit other sites about the show?***
Never
Rarely
Sometimes
Often
Always
Italy ($M = 3.19$); New Zealand ($M = 2.47$).

online discussions about the shows[28] and to download series-related applications[29] more than New Zealanders do.

Official Websites

Levene's Test	Significance	T	Degrees of Freedom	Significance (Two-Tailed)
32.854	0.000	10.772	499.810	0.000

Alternative Websites

Levene's Test	Significance	T	Degrees of Freedom	Significance (Two-Tailed)
3.233	0.072	8.835	359.921	0.000

Online Discussions

Levene's Test	Significance	T	Degrees of Freedom	Significance (Two-Tailed)
19.894	0.000	3.589	441.120	0.000

Downloading of Applications

Levene's Test	Significance	T	Degrees of Freedom	Significance (Two-Tailed)
39.307	0.000	4.669	461.539	0.000

---

[28] ***Do you participate in forum discussions about the show?***
  Never
  Rarely
  Sometimes
  Often
  Always
  Italy (M = 1.73); New Zealand (M = 1.47).

[29] ***Have you ever downloaded some of the show's applications or played the online games?***
  Never
  Rarely
  Sometimes
  Often
  Always
  Italy (M = 1.68); New Zealand (M = 1.40).

When it comes to the practice of purchasing items related to the series,[30] however, the *T*-test results indicate that, on average, New Zealanders tend to buy series-related merchandise more than the Italians.

Purchasing of Merchandise				
Levene's Test	Significance	T	Degrees of Freedom	Significance (Two-Tailed)
5.082	0.024	−6.932	112.600	0.000

T-TEST RESULTS FOR THE MAIN VARIABLE "SHOW"

The following trends represent the significant differences between the followers of *Game of Thrones* and the followers of *Mad Men* highlighted by the *T*-test results with regard to the main variable "Show."

The *T*-test indicates that, on average, the followers of *Game of Thrones* display a more significant form of engagement in external activities related to the show than the followers of *Mad Men*. This appears to be the case with reference to practices such as visiting alternative websites about the series,[31] downloading applications[32] and purchasing items related to the shows.[33]

---

[30] ***Have you ever bought any of the following items: books, DVDs and/or other merchandise that is associated with the show's name?***
Yes, I have
No, I have not
New Zealand (M = 2.06); Italy (M = 1.11).

[31] ***Do you visit other sites about the show?***
Never
Rarely
Sometimes
Often
Always
Game of Thrones (M =3.12); Mad Men (M = 2.55).

[32] ***Have you ever downloaded some of the show's applications or played the online games?***
Never
Rarely
Sometimes
Often
Always
Game of Thrones (M = 1.66); Mad Men (M = 1.39).

[33] ***Have you ever bought any of the following items: books, DVDs and/or other merchandise that is associated with the show's name?***
Yes, I have
No, I have not
Game of Thrones (M = 1.25); Mad Men (M = 0.93).

Alternative Websites

Levene's Test	Significance	T	Degrees of Freedom	Significance (Two-Tailed)
6.826	0.009	5.818	216.005	0.000

Downloading of Applications

Levene's Test	Significance	T	Degrees of Freedom	Significance (Two-Tailed)
25.962	0.000	3.933	255.282	0.000

Purchasing of Merchandise

Levene's Test	Significance	T	Degrees of Freedom	Significance (Two-Tailed)
102.041	0.000	4.866	438.046	0.000

CONCLUSIONS

The results of the statistical tests (chi-squared and T-test) outline a scenario in which specific habits of consumption are in fact relatable to the two nationalities under consideration. In this regard, the main differences between Italy and New Zealand have to do with the viewing process as a practice that takes place under particular conditions and within a certain timeframe, as well as to the engagement in activities related to the shows (i.e., following social media discussions, producing original material). As a main trend, people from New Zealand choose the evening as the preferred timeframe for watching the programs. The evening period emerges as the timeframe of preference for the Italians as well, but for the respondents from Italy, other parts of the day (in particular, the afternoon followed by the morning) also represent valid moments for the viewing activity. During the actual time of viewing, Italian people tend not to engage in parallel activities and prefer watching the programs by themselves more than New Zealanders do. In this sense and as a general tendency, Italian respondents appear to be more focused on viewing as a singular activity than those from New Zealand. On the other hand, the respondents from New Zealand engage more in the practice of binge-watching than the Italians. In terms of various platforms employed for watching the shows' episodes, the quantitative tests did not point out a significant difference between Italy and New Zealand with regard to the use of the traditional medium—that is, the television set. Nonetheless, with reference to other technological devices, Italians make more use of the tablet and mobile phone, whereas New Zealanders prefer the computer.

The level of engagement in online activities related to the programs also comes out as different when the corresponding results of the tests are combined together. As a dominant trend, Italian respondents display a higher level of interest in the practice of following updates (but mainly without posting[34]), taking part in discussions and visiting websites about the series more than New Zealanders, who in this regard appear to be less active. As for the modes of consumption that are dependent on the series of choice—*Game of Thrones* versus *Mad Men*—the main trends point to the fact that, in the case of *Game of Thrones*, followers remain up to date with viewing the aired episodes, are more prone to engaging in external activities related to the show (i.e., visiting websites, downloading applications, purchasing merchandise) and follow the online updates on the social media pages. In comparison, the followers of *Mad Men* display a significant lower level of interest in this set of practices, especially with reference to the online posts and updates regarding the series. This distinction calls attention to a potential correlation between media texts (like TV series) or even genres, and basic patterns that identify specific habits and behaviors in the modes of engagement. In particular, when it comes to texts that have been conceived as enlarged universes for an all-encompassing experience, fans' level of investment in the different elements of these universes stands as a direct evaluation of the efficiency of trans-media as a narrative strategy. But it also helps to identify those fictional story-worlds that appear to be more adaptable to a range of narrative investments, and hence to serve fans' needs for an immersive experience that sends them back to the core text. In the case of this study, the results of the quantitative analysis identify *Game of Thrones* as a TV show with more substantial potential for trans-media practices than *Mad Men*. But this raises the further question about the underlying motivations and concerns that encourage fans to adopt practices that match these different types of involvement. The focus group sessions permitted direct conversations with Italian and New Zealand fans of both shows, asking about their opinions, beliefs and experiences of these relevant matters,

---

[34] The posting of content emerges as an erratic and secondary activity, and even when it happens, it does not reach the level of a consolidated habit.

so as to acquire a better understanding of the dynamics that pertain to meaningful encounters between consumers of these texts and the media texts themselves. The following chapters integrate the answers that fans provided within
a framework that offers a theoretical explanation and justification for the distinct forms of media consumption and engagement identified here.

Chapter 4

THE PECULIARITIES OF *MAD MEN* AND *GAME OF THRONES* IN THE TRANS-MEDIA ECOSYSTEM

MAD MEN

"If you don't like what is being said, change the conversation"[1]—this is Don Draper's master rule for managing conflictual interactions with people at a dialogic level. In the *Mad Men* world, this process usually requires the capacity to shift the perspective from which an idea, a discourse or a fact is approached so as to attract one's interlocutor(s) toward a terrain that is familiar, safe. In a world of this kind, populated by individuals who have mastered the art of persuasion (and manipulation), the meaning of things—ranging from words uttered to acts performed and feelings experienced—is not apparent, but rather stratified, hidden among the many layers that constitute the nuances of human behavior. An intricate world, it needs to be followed with attention, processed, interpreted and reinterpreted. A TV series that turns on this paradigm may well be a "difficult" text for its viewers, but both the popularity of the show and the participants in this study suggest that viewers are attracted by the challenge, finding in the complexity of the storylines and characters' profiles a potent stimulus for dedicated viewing. With *Mad Men*, therefore, it is essential to start from the text, from the themes, visual attributes and human portraits that enliven the fabric of its story-world, so as to properly understand the emotional responses that the program is capable of generating and that, in turn, substantially impact on fans' modes of engagement with this show. In this chapter, the characteristics of *Mad Men* are examined through focus group participants' comments on the various textual elements that contribute to the series' fascination, both in terms of its accurate historical recreation and subtlety of the narrative.

---

[1] Don Draper, *Mad Men*, S03E02.

ADVERTISING THE 1960s: THE NOTION OF "NOSTALGIA"

Let's start from the title. In the first place, "Mad Men" stands for "the *Men of Mad*ison Avenue." In the story-world of the show, Madison Avenue identifies the street, in New York City, where the most important advertising agencies had their offices and headquarters from the late 1950s. Hence, the expression—coined by the executives themselves in the postwar period—refers to the men who worked in the advertising industry in Manhattan in that specific period. But "Mad Men" can also be interpreted in a more grammatical sense, in which case the first word is used as an attribute of the second one, and the expression calls attention to a sort of emotional state or attitude that signifies craziness, but in unspecified terms. To paraphrase the most famous tagline of the series—"*Mad Men*: Where The Truth Lies"—this is precisely where the ambiguity lies because, in its apparent simplicity, the title *Mad Men* is exemplary of the ambivalence that characterizes both the show's internal functioning and the way(s) it is viewed.

The historical period in which the story is set—the so-many-times-recalled-and-analyzed 1960s—marked the beginning of a new way of living and thinking, especially in the United States, thanks to the advent of new technologies, the rise of television and advertising, and new opportunities for women and minorities. This era of social and cultural upheaval is referred to as pivotal in the development of society, particularly in terms of the redefinition of traditional gender roles and social values. Involving years of massive turmoil at home and abroad, the 1960s eventually came to be seen as the epitome of radical change, exemplary of how sociocultural transformations develop and reshape societal structures. Considered "one of the most important decades in American cultural history" (Booker and Batchelor 13), the "mythical 60s" have turned, at the same time, into an idealized past as well as a past to leave behind. From this perspective, the 1960s functions as an alluring topic for a serial narrative whose goal is to explore the complex links between historical events and personal experiences, and *Mad Men* fans underlined the fascination exerted by the on-screen version of this particular era:[2]

– "Mad Men *is set in a period that fascinates me.*" [IT]
– "Mad Men *is a sophisticated show, for the psychology of it and the depiction of the historical time.*" [NZ]

---

[2] All the English translations of fans' comments are mine. The quotes from the focus groups have been selected on the basis of their relevance to the topics under discussion. The notations NZ and IT in brackets indicate, respectively, a comment uttered by a New Zealand fan and a comment uttered by an Italian fan.

– *"I like the historical representation in* Mad Men *because it adds realism to the story, and it makes the viewing more involving and satisfying."* [IT]
– *"I liked* Mad Men *for the story but also because the historical elements in it are significant. This aspect of the narrative makes the viewing of the show more appealing, more interesting."* [IT]

Advertising is not a random choice as the working environment for the people in the *Mad Men* world, and it emerged as notably interesting for the viewers:

– *"I liked* Mad Men *for the depiction of an industry I did not know that much about. I think that the representation of this historical time was well done, and I enjoyed watching it because it was stimulating."* [NZ]
– *"For me it was appealing because it explores advertising in the '60s, something that is hardly touched upon at all by any other mass media."* [NZ]

In the show, the advertising industry stands as a symbol of a society increasingly driven by the logic of capitalism and consumerism, while also referring to the visual and verbal discourses that substantiate that same logic and its sociocultural implications. In postwar American society, with the rise of television and the idea of consumption being equated to patriotism (Booker and Batchelor 20), advertising became the means of not just promoting goods and services but also "sell[ing] America, as the government sought to create a Cold War consensus at home and a positive image abroad" (Booker and Batchelor 21). Strictly intertwined with the set of "positive image[s]" that soon turned into a paradigm for the American lifestyle, the practice of advertising reveals itself as a potent metaphor for human existence, particularly in a capitalist, consumerist-driven society. In this regard, show-runner Matthew Weiner openly explained that the use of advertising in *Mad Men* is instrumental to develop a discourse, in the form of a metaphor, on the human condition. Booker and Batchelor note that the show itself "is a kind of a powerful advertisement for American life in the 1960s" (121), since it recreates an era in the form of a seductive object, while simultaneously reflecting on this complex operation of visual and narrative recreation.

   The triumph of the show is the way that the past is reconstructed, and literally re-presented with extreme accuracy, in a fictional drama written in the present. This double temporality translates into a tension that informs the whole narrative of the show, from the characters' storylines to the depiction of an era that promotes contradictory feelings in the audience. For those who yearn to go back to the 1960s, for instance, the nostalgia that the show induces can be defined in terms of "positive nostalgia," especially when it thrives on the seductiveness of visual elements like the dresses, the ornaments and the settings: "*Mad Men* satiates our yearning, inviting us to marvel at and enjoy the fashion, style, and historical accuracy of the program. [...] we are transported to a past that is undeniably shimmering and seductive" (Ciasullo 14–15). On a similar note, Heidi Brevik-Zender underlines the importance of garments for attracting audiences and allowing them to access a past that is generally presented in an idealized form: "In this way the world that the series depicts becomes a place where we as spectators ache to go (again), even knowing, as we do, that this can never occur" (Brevik-Zender 43). Fans also admitted the potency of the images and mise-en-scène that sustain the *Mad Men* historical recreation:

– *"The show is just beautifully made, beautifully shot [...] The sets are beautiful, the costumes are beautiful, I'm really attracted to the look of that time!"* [NZ]
– *"In watching* Mad Men *you can appreciate the cinematography, and the editing, and the costuming. There are so many elements that were far more than just the storylines."* [NZ]
– *"The historical period in which* Mad Men *is set makes the show more realistic, even if the representation preserves an imaginary aura."* [IT]

However, nostalgia is not reduced to the attractiveness of the style and ambience reproduced in the series. The alluring visual surface is just one of the multiple components of the appealing *Mad Men* universe:

– *"I don't think that there are people who have watched* Mad Men *throughout seven seasons due to the fact that 'Oh, Don Draper is so handsome!' or 'Oh, Joan is so hot!' [...] No, I don't believe that. Because the series would have been quite boring after a while for such superficial individuals."* [IT]

In the show, nostalgia becomes a means for investigating human beings' conflictual attitude toward the past. In *Mad Men and Politics*, Beail and Goren observe, "Nostalgia, indeed. The show has created a longing for 'stylish chaos' and 'wild pleasure' in this past, a past that our 'better, saner' selves know they do not really want to go back to and live in. But oh how we wish we could visit—or maybe just be photographed there" (Beail and Goren 8). This statement reveals the contrasting attitudes that *Mad Men* viewers are likely to adopt in relating to the series—a constant moving backward and forward between appreciation and distancing:

– *"I am really attracted to the look of the era, and I love the furniture and the dresses, and I would be fully happy to look like a woman in the 1960s all the time but I wouldn't actually want to be a woman in the 1960s [...] So, I feel like it's nostalgic for the look and the aesthetics of the 1960s, but it still shows aspects of the social reality that might generate more critique than nostalgia."* [NZ]

Clearly, a univocal illustration of the era is not what the show aims for. As Dunn, Manning and Stern point out, the show "functions as a literal time machine. But many aspects of its authenticity—the sexism, homophobia, and racism, for example—make the viewers' voyage an uncomfortable one" (Stern, Manning and Dunn 3). In this passage, the authors borrow the words uttered by Don Draper, the charming and mysterious protagonist of the series to illustrate the strategy according to which the ambivalence of *Mad Men* works. The reference to nostalgia as a "time machine" is extrapolated one of the most famous (and analyzed) sales pitches crafted by the talented Don in the course of the whole program, The Kodak Carousel Campaign.[3] In the final episode of the first season, the representatives of the Eastman Kodak Company arrive at the Sterling Cooper offices to listen to the ad campaign that the creative director has prepared for promoting the company's newest product: a slide projector named "The Wheel." During the scene, Don uses the technology itself to show a series of pictures of his family life: simple portraits of everyday existence that evoke fundamental concepts such as love, trust, acceptance, security. In commenting on the photos, Don provides an impressive lesson in great advertising by disclosing the benefit that the hitherto unknown and undesired technological device is meant to provide, in this case reliving memories of the past. "This device isn't a spaceship, it's a time machine," he explains. "It goes backwards, forwards, and takes us to a place where we ache to go again. It's not called the Wheel, it's the Carousel." In pointing out the dynamic that regulates the sentiment of nostalgia—a notion employed by Draper at the very beginning of the meeting as the premise of his presentation—the Carousel pitch translates into a meta-discourse about the series itself and its own characters. As Elisabeth Bronfen notes, "The work of fantasy is itself predicated on jumping backwards and forwards in time. It seeks to replace current discontent with memory images of the past that are themselves already conceived as a correction of the past" (Bronfen 53).

This is precisely what *Mad Men* does; the text corrects the past or, more specifically, offers the past in an altered version, in many respects alluring and captivating: "*Mad Men*'s evocation of the look of the 1960s [...] is a representation

---

[3] On the significance of this advertising campaign in relation to the show itself, Booker and Batchelor note, "For the *Mad Men* franchise, the carousel scene symbolizes the zenith of powerful writing, direction, style, and setting, culminating in overt audience outreach by appealing to viewers' nostalgic notions of the Camelot era" (Booker and Batchelor 133). For a detailed analysis of this scene, see also Bronfen (48–57).

not of the way the 1960s actually looked so much as of our cultural *memory,* half a century later, of the way the 1960s looked" (Booker and Batchelor 15). This misconception—or, better, fantasy—about the past is at the core of the nostalgic attitude: memory longs for an "idealized" version of what is forever gone. The series, from its first season, subtly calls attention to the use of nostalgia both as the *content* of its narrative and as the *form* of its representation. The sentiment finds in advertising a potent vehicle of expression due to the fact that it focuses on generating desire for elusive objects that are generally presented in a way that make them highly enticing. Indeed, in evoking nostalgia among the audience (both diegetic and non-diegetic) during his most famous pitch, Don Draper advertises himself as a person who has mastered creativity, is professionally charismatic and has a concrete understanding of the feelings he is talking about. Nevertheless, given the background of his childhood,[4] it is doubtful whether Don is actually capable of experiencing those specific emotions at this point: "Don's nostalgia is another parlor trick, created by an ad man to sell himself to a world in which he does not fit" (Booker and Batchelor 135). What is important to note is his conscious exploitation of those sentiments to sell an idea of himself that can be accepted and recognized by society as an image of success. Don's ability to constantly reinvent himself according to the specific situation and the expectations of those around him recalls the show's central theme of identity construction and social masks. It reinforces the idea of deception/manipulation as a subtle form of advertising that affects not only the presentation of goods and services but that of human beings as well.

HIDDEN IDENTITIES AND SOCIAL MASKS

In his article "The Time Machine: The History of Mad Men," James Poniewozik describes the AMC historical drama as "a serial about secrets: stolen identities and secret pregnancies and office intrigues. It's a love story, and sometimes a hate story" (Poniewozik). Indeed, as much as *Mad Men* is a period piece, it is also a show about what is hidden, and internalized. In this multilayered universe of emotions and feelings, men and women are expected to conform to unwritten rules of behavior and attend duties specifically designated for their gender. In the constant attempt to reconcile personal impulses and desires with the expectations dictated by institutions like the family, the company and society in general, *Mad Men* characters tend to repress their wants and inclinations in order to conform to a status that can ensure broad acceptance

---

[4] For a detailed analysis of Don Draper's personality, see Mattenson Mundt and Ward (108–16).

and recognition. In behaving in this way, *Mad Men* protagonists manage to establish a precarious balance between their authentic selves and the roles they choose to play in the different contexts of their lives, as was recognized by the focus group participants:

- *"Everybody in the show have their own fascination, they are damaged people."* [NZ]
- *"All charismatic characters in* Mad Men *have an oscillating personality; I am not saying that they are bipolar but almost. They know how to adapt to different situations."* [IT]
- *"The screenplay of* Mad Men *is designed to make you be revolted by some characters and their behaviour, but also be interested in what is going to happen to them."* [NZ]

In the diegetic context, characters' identities become manifest as the result of acts and temperaments that are aligned with what is expected and recognized as appropriate. But these are social masks, reworked versions of their true selves: the versions that they choose to project as their winning images in order to fit within the world(s) they inhabit. What they do, in the end, is essentially to engage in false advertising of themselves.[5]

Don Draper, the main protagonist of the show, is the embodiment of this peculiar form of deception. As an individual who has mastered creativity and is profoundly charismatic, Don reveals himself as strategically adaptable, someone capable of reinventing himself according to the specific situations and the expectations of the people he comes in contact with:

> We are not only drawn to Don's charismatic charm because he succeeds in winning our confidence, but also because we want to be taken in by his seductive play. Don's own self-confidence [...] thrives on the fact that he allows himself to be carried away by the force of his seductive inventions as well. By giving a shape and a name to the fantasies of others, he always also speaks about—and to—himself. (Bronfen 38)

This seductive power is capable of eliciting both positive and negative feelings in the viewers, and reveals Don as the epitome of the logic that substantiates the relation between advertising, American values and social relations in this nostalgic 1960s—"a true everyman for the modern world" (Booker and Batchelor 3):

---

[5] On the idea of crafting a successful image to be sold to the world, David Marc notes about the character of Don Draper, "Dick Whitman-as-Don Draper is a life as an advertising campaign: a child spawned in the lost America of love drapes himself in the trapping of a gentle man to sell himself to the world" (Marc 231–32).

— *"I'd like to be like Don because he is decisive and determined, not just charming, and he is also mysterious."* [IT]
— *"I think that Don Draper is a very self-confident character, he can intercept people's needs and desires."* [IT]

The fundamental ambiguity on which the character's identity is built explains the nature of Don's fascination, even though this ambivalence is underlined by the audience's contrasting feelings toward the series' male protagonist:

— *"Don is a great chameleon, he is very charismatic! And like all charismatic characters he knows how to adapt, he knows how to wear his masks."* [IT]
— *"Don is a very versatile character who manages to solve all the different situations with a sort of determination that only few people have. He knows how to adjust his behaviour, and I do appreciate him for this because he does what I am not capable of doing."* [IT]
— *"I find Don a negative character, fundamentally self-destructive both in his profession and personal life… I would never want to be like him!"* [IT]
— *"Don's life is such a performance! He performs to add up, to hide; I found him fascinating in the way that you can find a psychopath fascinating. There was so much so wrong with him from a psychological point of view, he is so dysfunctional! You keep asking yourself: 'Who else is he going to damage along the way?'"* [NZ]

The nature of Don's con game—the game that is the epitome of (m)ad men—comes out both as a form of manipulation and as a condition of the human subject, since we are all constrained by having to oscillate between acts of appearance and the need for authenticity. This is also the point where nostalgia originates: in the mismatch between factuality and what could have been (but is lost forever). And for Don, nostalgia will always be a "twinge in the heart,"[6] a restless quest for something that can only exist in an idealized form, like an imaginary childhood perceived as a time of unconditional love and appreciation. Quite significantly, Don's nostalgia for a past that he has only experienced in the form of an unachievable desire is the element that humanizes the character in the eyes of the spectators, since it allows them to come in contact with the vulnerability that lies beneath the surface of his emotional detachment:

— *"Don Draper is a character who wants the fiction to become the reality. He can't live his inner life and he thinks that it is just the same for all the others."* [IT]
— *"Don is compelling and awful at the same time!"* [NZ]

---

[6] Don Draper, *Mad Men*, S01E13.

– *"This individual who appears to be so self-confident in the end reveals his fragility, he shows different facets of his personality."* [IT]

Other characters' stories are exemplary of false advertising as a strategy for delivering an image of themselves divergent from their true identities. Betty Draper-Francis, the first wife of Don Draper, systematically disguises her state of profound discontent by displaying an apparent condition of happiness. From the very beginning, Betty's character is represented as part of an ideal picture that on the screen is constructed as immaculate and fascinating. Visual signifiers of this perfection are her stylish dresses, her flawless appearance as the "trophy wife," her poses and general attitude within the household that is portrayed as a small reign of order and serenity:

– *"Betty is the 'trophy' wife, she represents the classic '50s -'60s femininity of a certain class; she is used to be admired and looked at."* [NZ]

Betty's capacity to properly fit this role—from the gestures to the style choices—originates from her working experience as a model. From this perspective, Betty's physical appearance designates that her personality is constructed from a process of altered, remodeled images. In proposing herself as the gorgeous wife and mother of three, Betty takes active part in the advertising campaign initiated together with her husband Don, which is inseparable from their self-representation as the "ideal" American family. Of course, the series aims at systematically dismantling this image of completeness through the accumulation of narrative elements that point out Betty's exasperation and state of misery. The heavy drinking and smoking, the shaking of her hands, the need to see a psychiatrist are all symptoms of a situation more and more difficult to handle: "Through Betty's story, we see the discontent of the suburban housewife and, through her character, we also see Friedan's warnings in *The Feminine Mystique* that a woman groomed for nothing but domesticity is doomed [...] to a life of existential unhappiness" (Marcovitch and Batty 11). Labeled as fundamentally narcissistic and petulant ("Worst Characters on TV,"), Betty is the *Mad Men* character that, as a general trend, fans love to hate:[7]

– *"Betty seemed to me to represent the sort of audience that Marilyn French's book,* The Woman's Room, *was directed at. Betty's lifestyle is very much the same lifestyle that Marilyn French describes in her book, that is about four women trapped in their gendered roles."* [NZ]

---

[7] "Fans took perverse delight in Betty's terrible parenting" (Spiro and Lawler 60).

— *"Betty went from being a petulant teenager to being a wife. She is an awful mother, she's so mean to her kids, she's insufferable and whines all the time about nothing!"* [NZ]
— *"I don't think that Betty is a very contemporary character because she's just a housewife, and as for today it is not realistic to think in terms of a nuclear family with three kids where only one person goes to work and has a salary!"* [IT]
— *"I feel like stuff happens to Betty rather than Betty herself developing. She doesn't seem to have that much agency."* [NZ]
— *"Usually, we tend to identify with strong personalities which means that, in my opinion, no one would dare to say "I'd like to be Betty!" because she's quite weak."* [IT]

Nevertheless, some fans expressed compassion for Betty's suffering as well as conviction that her personality calls attention to the fact that, at closer look, Don's first wife is a more complex character than what she appears to be:

— *"To be honest, I felt pretty awful for Betty the whole time [...] I could tell why she reacted in a lot of ways to all the situations."* [NZ]
— *"I think that Betty's personality is revealed when she writes that letter to her daughter, after she finds out she has cancer. Betty is not stupid and she has chosen a path that has made her a detestable character, but it has never been easy for Betty. It is very easy being a successful individual when you have success, like Don does; it is much more difficult being Betty, I mean: someone capable of being so consistent with the choices she has made up until the end."* [IT]

In contrast to Betty, Peggy Olson is a single girl who feels the need to have a career and is not prone to taking advantage of her sexuality as a means of persuasion. Indeed, she "defies the designated roles for white women in early 1960s America. Furthermore [...] she also possesses impressive managerial talent" (Lehman 159). Peggy refuses to be defined as just a "type," she refuses to be "relegated to being either the 'Jackie' or the 'Marilyn.'" (Farrell 33), or as a mere object of male desire, or as a future somebody's wife whose only aspiration is to move to a beautiful house in the suburbs. An anti-Betty in many respects, Peggy finds herself "disconnected" from her body when she is incapable of acknowledging her pregnancy and rejects a baby that is seen as an insurmountable obstacle to building a successful career.[8] Like Don, she conceals a private occurrence that might do damage to the image of devoted and zealous worker that she uses as her form of personal advertising. Peggy

---

[8] Matthew Weiner explains the reason for Peggy's problematic relation with her body, in particular with reference to the pregnancy: "I wanted to do a story about a woman getting fat because she couldn't deal with being sexualized all the time [...] She becomes a guy, and they give her a big punch in her shoulder. She makes it." (Witchel).

finds power in the use of personal attributes—mainly, her brain—that are not those to which men are accustomed to in their interactions with women. For this reason, her actions emerge as highly significant in the show's delineation of the evolution of gender relations and women's roles: "Though her male counterparts often trivialize her ideas, Peggy continues to manipulate even as she is manipulated, using her presence and voice within the male sphere to alter perceptions of women in and out of the workplace" (Marotte 35).

Peggy's efforts to succeed at her job, her compromises between the work and her personal life, and her confrontations with the kind of sexism that still exists today in the working environment make her the character through which the series manages to speak in both the present and the past tense. According to Marcovitch and Batty, she "is the female character representing the diachronic viewing of the show, bridging the early sixties with the feminist movements of the later sixties and early seventies and finally with the working women of the early twenty-first century" (13). The majority of fans recognize in Peggy the character who succeeds in asserting her liberation from the constraints of a sexist culture, who makes the difference by carrying out a radical change in terms of professional advancement and personal attitude:

– *"The character of Peggy is very interesting to me for the way she evolves."* [NZ]
– *"I find Peggy a winning character, who manages to have a career and to find her own place in a hostile working environment, and without giving in to the excesses that characterize both Don's and Roger's behaviour!"* [IT]

But Peggy's evolutionary process comes at a very personal high cost, since she feels the necessity to put her sentimental life on hold for quite some time in order to actively pursue a career in the industry. *Mad Men* never stops reminding its audience of the historical as well as contemporary demands on women who want to find a compromise between their femininity and their value as individuals deserving of equal opportunities in patriarchal contexts:

– *"The series definitely makes you think about how far we've come, how far women have come."* [NZ]
– *"It is kind of just funny, at some point, how sexist these situations are; and it's very interesting to see the progression and then reflect on it in your own life."* [NZ]

In the end, Peggy seems to be the (only) one who really "has it all," but it is worth noting that her storyline's resolution, marked by the beginning of a serious relationship with her colleague Stan Rizzo, was perceived as a setback by some fans with regard to the promise of full independence and self-realization that she was supposed to carry out:

– *"I found the final episode really disappointing with Peggy... She's going to be happy because she realized she's actually in love, and that really annoyed me!"* [NZ]

In the world of *Mad Men*, the lives of Don, Betty and Peggy epitomize the internal struggles that people have to face while looking for their place in the world. This existential quest emerges as an essential need, and transports viewers beyond the occurrences of a specific historical period so as to create a profound resonance with the lives of individuals in the contemporary era.

MAD MEN'S TRUTH: BETWEEN NOSTALGIA FOR "A PLACE THAT CANNOT BE" AND DESIRE FOR A TIME THAT IS YET TO COME

Mad Men is entirely built on a trajectory of intersecting temporalities, where past and present reference each other, and the characters emerge as individuals whose lives are in many ways similar to those of the people who watch the show: "Real history enters into the past of a fictional world that Matthew Weiner historically reimagined from the position of his own present, even as it leads us back into our contemporary moment" (Bronfen 172). The mixture of individuals' professional challenges and internal conflicts, intertwined in turn with the processes of social change, contributes to the attraction that the series exerts in terms of realism and historical verisimilitude:

– *"I like the characters' progression along with the representation of the social changes."* [NZ]
– *"The characters evolve, change, go back in life, and this is one of the positive things in the series."* [IT]

It gradually becomes apparent that everything in *Mad Men* always means something else (Stoddart 11), and offers multiple interpretations. Indeed, what we are constantly reminded of is that many of the driving ideas and powerful slogans created in the 1960s to justify the legitimacy of basic notions—such as the ideal American family and the American Dream—were, essentially, the product of effective advertising. If in the beginning, when James Truslow Adams employed the expression for the first time in his book *The Epic of America* (1931), the American Dream referred to "the freedom people had to determine their place in the world" (Booker and Batchelor 24) subsequently "as the decades of the mid-twentieth century unfolded, [...] *the American Dream soon became entangled with broader notions of what is meant to be successful in a capitalist system*" (Booker and Batchelor 24; my emphasis). In this regard, the America of the 1960s as the content of *Mad Men* becomes symbolic of a period that had a worldwide resonance (via, for instance, popular culture narratives) and that, simultaneously, preserved a specificity that belongs to the American nation, its traditions and cultural values. Indeed, the first two quotes in the following grouping point out how the Italian fans position themselves as removed from the American culture. The ambivalence here lies in the realization that the 1960s represents both a nationally *specific* and a globally (across the West) *shared* historical past—that is, a precise extent of time in the history of the United States as well as a period whose historical events have had international socio-cultural repercussions and influences:

- *"I found the series very representative of the 'American style' [...] It is interesting because it represents a different world; I think that if they had presented the same story, set in the same period in Italy, it would have been way less interesting for us! I liked the setting and the characters, and things like the costumes and the hairstyles too."* [IT]
- *"The American events of that time have not been experienced by us in the same way they have been experienced by the American people."* [IT]
- *"Even if the events represented in* Mad Men *are from the American history, they are events that had an international resonance, like the Kennedy assassination and the presidential campaigns."* [IT]

The practice of promoting desirable objects, even sociopolitical objects, via the benefits that these objects seem to guarantee eventually turned the notion of happiness into an endless purchasing practice whose ultimate object is, by definition, unattainable. The final goal is to keep the desire for the new always alive, to the point that the condition of "striving for" (something, someone, someplace) becomes the only possible status, the paradigm of living.

In this sense, advertising stands as the emblem of the fundamental ideology of the American nation: the American Dream. Elisabeth Bronfen illustrates the characteristics of the American Dream as the promise of "a new beginning after the old world has fallen apart [...] The collapse of one world emerges as the precondition for the recovery of another world, which is to say for a new beginning" (Bronfen 15). For a new beginning to happen, change is mandatory. It becomes a lasting condition of the American subject who "must justify his or her right to happiness over and over again" (Bronfen 22). In making the idea of reinvention part of a constant pursuit of happiness, the risk is the creation of a misleading and unproductive attitude: "What one is enthralled with is the force of the American dream, not its concrete realization. What one desires is the act of striving, not the goal to be achieved" (Bronfen 24). The unattainable condition on which the American Dream thrives helps us to understand the recurring state of dissatisfaction and incompleteness enacted in *Mad Men*; only individuals who are permanently unsatisfied and constantly in pursuit of the new will embrace the logic of "striving for" as an existential rule. The main protagonists of *Mad Men* are all different versions of the American Dream. They abide by the logic of advertising by crafting respectable personal appearances that can make them feel accepted within the world they inhabit, while trying to deal with their longings for a role different than the one they are, for various reasons, forced to impersonate. In selling themselves as content and satisfied individuals, while experiencing the instability of a status that is never fully accomplished, *Mad Men* characters ultimately embody the ideal that substantiates the internal functioning of both advertising and the American Dream: happiness as an endlessly deferred promise.

Through this endless deferral, the series manages to thematize emotional instability and a sense of precariousness by constructing a reality that is highly nuanced and stratified. Indeed, the fascination peculiar to Matthew Weiner's series resides in the precision of its visual reconstructions and potency of scenes that are comparable to impeccable tableaux; they please the eye and illuminate the screen with seductive beauty. But beyond the alluring and glittering surfaces of the garments and accessories, when the camera moves back and the baubles are out of frame, these representations display a different reality, one that is less attractive and captivating: "Matthew Weiner's show is about the fact that the persuasion remains on the surface of the images—those produced by his advertisers and those he himself produces. Thus, to the end, sentimental bonding and ironic distance work hand in hand" (Bronfen 72–73). This fluctuation of emotions that the series manages to promote originates from the subtlety of its depiction, since "what *Mad Men* is brilliant at doing is that it places familiar tableaux in unfamiliar narratives" (Wilson and Lane Jr 81). Within these familiar tableaux, *Mad Men*'s detailed representation of the '60s is instrumental in highlighting, on one hand, the progress achieved historically in the matter of civil rights and gender relations. On the other, the "madness" (Marcovitch and Batty 9–10) of an age that is inherently turbulent, filled with dysfunctional relations, power struggles and discrimination, serves as a reminder of what the present is still like. In looking at the characters, from their seductive external appearances to their hidden desires and frustrations, what viewers are doing is basically looking at themselves, their lives and their own world: "However dated *Mad Men* seems on the surface [...] audiences are drawn to it because the story is fundamentally similar to ours" (Campbell 97). This point, which has been reiterated by scholars, was not lost on the focus group participants:

– *"Our period is very much like the sixties. Matthew Weiner has fundamentally decided to choose a fascinating vessel—that is, the 1960s in America—to address existential problems in the background of great epochal events. The series has the 'right distance' because it restrains the viewer from saying, 'No, it is too close to my reality, I do not want to see this, it confuses me and it's disturbing', but it still manages to deliver that message of reflection on reality that is what really matters."* [IT]

— *"During the viewing of* Mad Men, *I kept asking myself: aside from certain behaviours that are unacceptable for us today, what generates this sort of affection toward the show? In my opinion, it is the fact that what we see on the screen resonates with us because it deals with themes that are central to our own existence. It tells us a lot about our own identities, which are also liquid and fragile [...] And the women's struggles to have a career, to affirm their own value in a male-oriented society, are still relevant for us today. These things really impressed me, and I got the feeling that I have been growing with the characters through the years. It is the experience of life that stands at the core of* Mad Men *representation, and this is what makes this series so involving and cathartic."* [IT]

Multiple levels of discontent inform the fictional lives of the characters, who all feel, in different ways and for different reasons, disconnected from the place and time they inhabit. Correspondingly, diverse feelings emerge in those who watch the show. Wilson and Lane recognize *Mad Men*'s cathartic effect, noting that "What makes *Mad Men* so compelling is that we long for an ideal that we are simultaneously reminded was not real. [...] Watching *Mad Men* is cathartic because it allows us to confront this longing [...] But it also reminds us that we cannot 'go back' to a 'simpler time' because this time did not exist" (Wilson and Lane Jr. 83). Viewers find themselves caught in the middle of an ambivalent attraction for a desirable, yet unachievable, object—the re-created "good old days" that never really existed—undergirded by the uncertain appreciation of a present that is perceived as more advanced than what appears on the screen but is in many respects still very similar to it. Poniewozik puts it succinctly when he writes, "When we visit its time, [...] *we're visiting the same place we live,* even if you've never set foot in midtown Manhattan" (Poniewozik 2017; my emphasis). The present time becomes, from this perspective, the premise of something else, presumably better, that can only exist in the future: the (never-to-be-fully-accomplished) promise of absolute happiness. This is, after all, the truth that *Mad Men* chooses to tell. The only dimension where human beings can manage to exist is "in between": between nostalgia for "a place that cannot be" and desire for a time that is yet to come. In this in-between space, the era inhabited by the show's characters coalesces with the era inhabited by its audiences.

OFFICIAL TRANS-MEDIA STRUCTURE OF MAD MEN

The series' official website (http://www.amc.com/shows/mad-men) at the time of writing offers "pieces" of Don Draper's world, ranging from extra information on the cast, crew and production to games and interactive features. This material contributes to the re-creation of *Mad Men* "coolness" as part of a captivating process with which audiences can engage and perform creatively: "The series' web site which is filled with trivia quizzes, interviews, and blogs dedicated to the show helps to construct a community of 'shared experience', encouraging fans to contribute to the weekly exchange of ideas and 'become' Mad Men through the creation of Avatars" (Stoddart). The five main sections of the website—Episodes, Exclusives, Talk, Cast and Crew, About—are filled with a notable number of videos, news, quizzes, online conversations, interviews, merchandise, apps, photos, guides and bios of actors and characters.

In the "Episodes" section, under "Explore Episodes," all the episodes from Season 7 are grouped together and presented with detailed recaps, a collection of behind-the-scenes videos, interviews with members of the cast and a gallery of photos from the set. In the same section, the link "Where to Watch" allows access to a full archive of all AMC shows' past seasons, but in this area, the videos of the series' episodes are not accessible to viewers outside of the United States due to geographic restrictions as part of the cable policy. The same rule applies to the first two videos that appear at the top of the home page, *The Cast Bids a Fond Farewell to the Show* and *Cast and Creators Break Down the Series Finale*, which are positioned outside of the aforementioned sections; the videos display content related to the final season of the show, but are accessible only to viewers in the United States. The "Exclusives" section has been conceived mainly as an entertaining space. Fans can enjoy building their own *Mad Men* avatar from the ground up thanks to the interactive game "*Mad Men* Yourself," where it is possible to choose clothes and accessories that resemble the appearance of the *Mad Men* characters, while for women who are interested in trying the '60s look, the "Hair and Makeup Lookbook" provides accurate descriptions of the makeup and hair style selected by makeup department head Lana Horochowski and hair department head Theraesa Rivers. Fashion is also at the center of the detailed descriptions of the clothes from specific episodes presented in the guide "The Complete Fan Companion." Along a similar theme, the "Online Party Planner" is a guide rich in suggestions and external links to be used for important events, like throwing a party. This feature contains precise instructions on how to embellish a celebration, and enrich it with a particular *Mad Men* atmosphere. The "*Mad Men* Ultimate Fan Games" is meant for loyal followers who like demonstrating their wide and detailed knowledge of the series, whereas the "Which of Don's Women Are You?" test is for the female public: an imaginary date with Don Draper becomes the scenario for a woman to discover her corresponding fictional personality. The same approach applies to the "Which *Mad Men* Are You?" questionnaire, through which users can find out which *Mad Men* character they share the most similarities with, the main difference being that the character-user identifications are not based on gender.

A range of material provides fans with opportunities for transforming *Mad Men* into a real-world personalized experience, in particular through the integration of elements from its universe into people's everyday lives. The "Sterling Cooper & Partners Job Interview Game" simulates a hypothetical interview session for a vacancy at an important advertising company; the question list challenges the applicant's skills to meet the firm's requirements and to think according to a certain kind of mindset. In this section it is also possible to purchase show-related merchandise: the *Mad Men* Collector's Edition Barbie Dolls, music singles and soundtracks, DVD box sets of all the series' seasons and a range of books—*Mad Men: The Illustrated World*, *Mad Men: The Fashion File* and *Roger Sterling: Wit & Wisdom of an Ad Men*. The first one is conceived as a comprehensive anthology of the *Mad Men* era. It includes chapters on the offices, the houses, the concepts of fashion and beauty and what came to be considered "mainstream" versus "counterculture." In the second manual it is possible to find a detailed analysis of the characters' looks and suggestions on how to create a personalized style that follows the most popular dictates of fashion, while the third text offers a highly enter-taining portrayal of a single character, Roger Sterling, outlined through the assortment of his most caustic jokes and observations both on the advertising world and the human relationships in the 1960s. In addition to these items, wallpapers and screensavers with the images of the characters and the iconic Don Draper's silhouette from the title sequence are offered for downloading. The "Cocktail Culture" app is designed to be more demanding than simple quizzes: it questions players' skills at preparing popular cocktails from the '60s and it also provides feedback on the bartending abilities displayed during the game.

The show's allure, as represented by characters' suits and dresses, has also been a source of inspiration for many fashion brands and designers, like Michael Kors, Bloomingdale, Brooks Brothers, Banana Republic, who have paid homage to the *Mad Men* style with their dedicated collections and by establishing promotional partnerships with AMC. In 2009, the Hilton Hotels chain also contributed to the promotion of the series through the launch of the "Live Like a *Mad Man*" contest: the winner received two round-trip tickets to New York City, a *Mad Men* wardrobe item, a "*Mad Men* Guide to New York" and a DVD collection of the first two seasons. Moreover, for the "New York's Gone MAD" initiative in August 2009, fans had the chance to visit the actual locations in the city of New York, where it was possible to drink some of the most popular 1960s cocktails, as well as to attend the live screening of the first episode of Season 3 in Times Square at 11:00 p.m. The aim of all these features, applications and entertaining urban activities is to encourage fans to recreate spaces and social events through which they will be able to identify with the characters of the show by appropriating and transposing the *Mad Men* experience in their lives. AMC's senior marketing vice president Linda Schupack has explained the underlying logic of this web of diverse practices envisioned as a strategic exploitation of the *Mad Men* appeal: "'We knew we couldn't go a traditional route in marketing this show [...] We felt we needed to be provocative, confident, and bold' if we were to have 'a chance to rebrand the network with an intelligent, upscale series [...] Intelligent TV can sometimes be the hardest to market, relying more on critics and creative positioning'" (Edgerton 14).

On the home page of the AMC website, further sections that allow viewers to deepen the knowledge of the universe created by Matthew Weiner include the "Cast & Crew" section, which comprises full bios of the main protagonists in combination with an assortment of interviews with the actors and actresses. This section also contains a set of full portraits of the secondary characters; each portrait is enriched by a distinctive character's quote from the show. For example, Bertram Cooper's selected quote is "Who cares?"—the unexpected, and yet highly significant answer given to Pete Campbell, who had just revealed the truth about Don Draper's real identity. Another one is Don's lover Suzanne Farrell's "I know exactly how it ends," a sad reminder of the destructive relation pattern adopted by the protagonist throughout the whole series. As for the "Crew" subcategory, it focuses on the man behind *Mad Men*, creator Matthew Weiner. A full bio of the showrunner/producer chronicles his main achievements for *Mad Men* as well as the other shows he worked on as part of the production team. In a segment dedicated to five important moments from *Mad Men* Season 6, Weiner explains his inspirations for the creation of those significant events in the narrative. In the "About" area it is possible to find a written synopsis of the show with central information on the production and the cast and crew as well as two videos—the already mentioned *The Cast Bids a Fond Farewell to the Show* and the trailer "Nostalgia: *Mad Men* Season 7"; the latter is available to all viewers with no geographic restrictions. The "Talk" division comprises two distinct parts: "Blog" and "Forum." In the "Blog," an extremely rich collection of various articles—interviews, opinion pieces, press reviews with direct links to the magazines, analyses of the ad campaigns presented in the show—delve into the multiple layers of *Mad Men* storylines and representation. Each piece is shareable thanks to a direct link to the major social media sites (Facebook, Twitter, Reddit, Tumblr, Google+). The "Forum," on the other hand, is designed as an interactive space for online conversations among the fans of the series. All the sections of the site display a direct link to the two primary social media profiles of the show, Twitter and Facebook, under the category

"Follow *Mad Men*," while direct access to other AMC's original shows—such as, *Better Call Saul*, *The Night Manager*, *Turn: Washington Spies*—is located at the bottom of the various divisions under the title "More AMC Originals."

Alternative reference sources for those who are interested in or passionate about *Mad Men* are the popular blog named *Tom + Lorenzo: Fabolous and Opinionated* (http://tomandlorenzo.com/tag/mad-style/) and the website Mad Men Wiki (http://madmen.wikia.com/wiki/Mad_Men_Wiki). In the former, a gay couple offers accurate analyses of the latest fashion trends, ranging from celebrities' looks to movies and television shows' styles; as they describe themselves, "we're a full service pop culture site with a special focus on fashion and style with an audience in the millions." With regard to *Mad Men*, the site presents a rich archive of detailed commentaries on the significance of the colors, accessories, costumes and settings from the various episodes of the series. These "insanely detailed *Mad Men* recaps" that are meant to be "referenced by anyone looking to do a deep dive about the colors, clothes, and fashion history lessons of the swinging '60s" have gained large popularity for the blog, thanks to a critical approach that displays a refreshing and entertaining perspective on the aesthetic facets of such a complex TV program.

Mad Men Wiki is a free wiki hosting service that publishes for the most part user-generated content (http://www.wikia.com/about). It is a dedicated section of the website WIKIA (also known as FANDOM powered by Wikia), which was launched in 2006 by Jimmy Wales as the home of FANDOM, the biggest entertainment fan site in the world. The goal was to provide fans a virtual place to engage with and share their love for popular culture products with other fans. Indeed, through FANDOM, a fan can develop a wiki on any subject of interest, or can choose to take part in existing fan communities by contributing original content, or by initiating or joining a conversation. The *Mad Men*-related material that can be found on this site consists of (a) a collection of analyses of specific episodes (accompanied by various kinds of additional content, such as the cast list, trivia information, pithy quotes, a gallery of images, etc.); (b) an assortment of characters' profiles with multiple divisions for each profile; (c) a list of the *Mad Men* Cocktail Recipes with pictures (provided by amctv.com), with all the ingredients and the instructions for making the drinks and (d) detailed overviews of the series' seven seasons, enriched by a list of episode synopses and awards won by the program. The character profiles are of particular significance, since the information provided on each character is internally organized both in the form of a comprehensive biography[9] and a

---

[9] For instance, for the character of Don Draper the list comprises "Childhood," "Life in the Brothel," "Military Service," "A New Life," "Ad Man," "A New Company."

summary tab that displays the character's personal and professional information. Additional sections—such as "Women," "Quotes," "Clothing/Fashion
Style," "Office," "Gallery"—deal with other fundamental aspects of the
particular character's story, such as his/her romantic life and the distinctive fashion look displayed throughout the seasons of the show, with the last
point in particular subject to both analysis and illustration.

MAD MEN AND ITS "CENTRIPETAL COMPLEXITY"

In *Complex TV: The Poetics of Contemporary Television Storytelling* (2015), Jason
Mittell analyzes the main textual characteristics of different contemporary
TV shows in order to elucidate the notion of narrative complexity as peculiar to the plots and characterization of their stories. According to Mittell,
there are two main types of complexity that help us understand differences
in the shows' narratives: "centripetal" versus "centrifugal." Mittell uses
the example of *Breaking Bad* to list and explain the characteristics of the
first type of narrative complexity, "in which narrative movement pulls
actions and characters inward toward a gravitational center, establishing
a thickness of backstory and character depth that drives the action. The
effect is to create a story-world with unmatched depth of characterization,
layers of backstory, and psychological complexity building on viewers'
experiences and memories over the program's numerous seasons" (222–
23). In this explanation, the relevance given to the properties of the fictional story-world—"depth of characterization, layers of backstory, and
psychological complexity"—resonates with both New Zealand and Italian
fans' comments in describing the main traits that delineate the universe of
Mad Men, both in terms of character depictions and the intricacy of the
media text's storylines. In his analysis of "centripetal complexity," Mittell
also specifies,

> On *Breaking Bad*, there is always the sense that a marginal past
> event might get pulled back into the narrative center and impact
> Walt's fate in unpredictable but justifiable ways: this centripetal
> force creates a complex story-world that holds its main characters
> accountable for past misdeeds and refuses to let them (or us) escape
> these transgressions at the level of story consequences or internal
> psychology. (222–23)

With reference to *Mad Men*, this aspect of the narrative can be used to describe
the underlying dynamic of Don Draper's storyline, the character whose mysterious past represents one of the major enigmas in the development of the

plot. "Centrifugal complexity," on the other hand, refers to a different type of story,

> [one] in which the ongoing narrative pushes outward, spreading characters across an expanding story-world. On a centrifugal program, there is no single narrative center, as the action traces what happens between characters and institutions as they spread outward. It is not just that the series expands in quantity of characters and settings but that its richness is found in the complex, web of interconnectivity forged across the social system rather than in the depth of any one individual's role in the narrative or psychological layers. (222–23)[10]

This description of textual elements can be employed to illustrate the narrative structure that characterizes the convoluted cosmos of a text like *Game of Thrones*, with its cast of hundreds of characters and multiple settings, and a "web of interconnectivity" that develops across different social systems.

Both notions of narrative complexity illustrated by Mittell can also be employed to clarify the dynamics that regulate fans' modes of engagement with the expanded structures of the series. Indeed, the narrative strategy identified by Mittell as a metaphorical movement that, in one case, "pulls actions and characters inward toward a gravitational center" while in the other it "pushes [the narrative] outward," can also function as a useful indication of the distinct ways fans relate to the shows. For *Mad Men*, followers are attracted to a "center"—consisting of the storylines, characters' representation, internal rhythm and aesthetic qualities—that finds within the series the main source of interest and motivation for the viewing. As a show that displays a highly detailed depiction of a known era/society, as well as character portrayals that subtly delve into the psychology of each, the program in itself comes out as a text that does not require fans to go beyond the construction of its televisual content to be fully interpreted and appreciated. Rather, it demands forms of meditation that maintain fans' attention on the events and the protagonists inside that fictional frame. As a consequence of this type of involvement, the various media extensions that populate the expanded structure of the series do not appear so relevant for deepening fans' engagement with the text. Indeed, in the eyes of fans, the quizzes and the games, the interactive features and the applications, the online guides and the "cosplay" performances do not contribute much to the fictional reality of *Mad Men*, at least not in the terms that seem to matter the most to them. This additional material might elicit

---

[10] For the concept of "centrifugal complexity," the TV show referred to by Jason Mittell as the illustrative example is *The Wire* (HBO, 2002–8).

a generic attraction and interest, but what is worth noticing is that, for this particular show, the core content stands as the gravitational point that all fans tend to focus on and keep going back to, in ways that exemplify their predilection for a type of involvement that, in Mittell's terminology, tends to favor the main text at the expense of the various para-texts. In this regard, it is also significant that fans admitted to being more intrigued by fan-made content—mainly, entertaining YouTube videos—rather than by the assorted material proposed by the official source:

– *"I am more interested in the idea of appropriating a text, even in the form of a parody! For instance, on YouTube there is a video made with parts of scenes from* Mad Men *in which every single word is employed for the creation of the song 'Never Gonna Give You Up' [...] It might look absurd to know that someone came up with an idea like this one, but I am interested in the reception process of these media products. As for me, I did not make a lot: I cut and put together some scenes from the series in the guise of avatar and I posted them on my Facebook profile. I did this as a promotional strategy, since I wanted to initiate some of my contacts to the viewing of the series [...] Just simple things like this."* [IT]

However, the notion of text appropriation in terms of practices that self-consciously differ from the analysis and comprehension of the fictitious world did not turn out to be a major trend among the *Mad Men* fans.

When asked about the possibility of purchasing items related to the show, fans revealed,

– *"I feel like the shows that really generate lots of merchandising and cosplay are the sci-fi and fantasy shows, those with outlandish looks and worlds."* [NZ]
– *"I have seen the cups in store with the* Mad Men *logo, and I might buy them as a gift for someone who is really super into Mad Men. But for Mad Men there isn't much of this stuff."* [NZ]
– *"Are there purchasable items from the* Mad Men *world?"* [IT]
– *"I'd probably get an action figure of Don Draper, but I haven't seen a lot of* Mad Men *merchandise."* [NZ]

The recurring comparisons with *Game of Thrones*, through which fans disclosed their reasons for being involved in the shows in distinct ways, substantiates the theory according to which the nature of the texts' narrative impacts on fans' habits and attitudes. Fictional worlds that are built on centripetal directions of development seem to promote similar forms of interest and involvement. This means that fans become attracted to the show in a way that induces them to *move towards* the content of the episodes, so as to stay mainly focused on the characteristics of the text. For *Mad Men*, these textual characteristics are the historical recreation, characters' psychologies and style of the representation. On the other hand, features that are related to the series but belong to the network of media extensions do not stimulate fans' interest in the same way:

- *"Mad Men's fans are not very interested in games or quizzes; maybe they would be more intrigued by a different type of material, for instance retrospectives on the characters. This is also due to the fact that the target audience is more adult than those of other shows."* [IT]
- *"I have to say that I am not at all interested in a quiz like 'Which Mad Men Character Are You?'."* [IT]
- *"I am not interested in the cocktail guide or in the guide on how to throw a Mad Men party, and even with the 'Mad Men Yourself' interactive feature... I mean: once you have created the avatar, what's next? It's pretty much over."* [IT]
- *"Mad Men is a series that elicits inner reflections."* [IT]

"Inner reflections" do not require additional material to properly develop. If this is the case for *Mad Men*—as it appears to be, based on fans' statements—then a primary factor that deserves attention and consideration is fans' awareness regarding this dynamic. *Mad Men* followers identify themselves as part of a fandom that displays interest in television programs that promote a certain type of emotional investment in the show—in Don Draper's words, this would be defined as the "sentimental bond" with the product. This type of attachment has as its primary objective the appropriation of the text itself, not in the form of an exploration of its media extensions, but as a full understanding of its narrative nuances, subtexts and multiple storylines: "The range of intertextual reference anchors the program in the era, but also extends well beyond this to address the show's contemporary, media savvy audience" (White 154). In short, it is the notion of so-called quality television[11] that matters the most to *Mad Men* fans:

- *"I think that the fandom of* Mad Men *is different from a fandom that involves fan fiction and cosplay performances, and it is also about this idea of 'quality television' that defines you with regards to the idea of being a certain type of fan. 'This is going to be me,' because it is the kind of television that I choose to watch, even if I do not dress up as a woman from the '60s!"* [NZ]

As a predominant trait of the text, this concept also validates the theory that what drives these fans, what keeps them interested and engaged, lies within the series itself. The consequence is a notable lessening of the relevance that

---

[11] For a detailed analysis of this concept, see Mittell 210–26.

the network of para-texts plays in the development, and preservation, of fans'
attraction to the TV program.

What does all this entail for trans-media? According to Mittell,

> trans-media extensions might provide an additional revenue stream, but
> their primary function is to drive viewers back to the television series; for
> creators, trans-media storytelling must always support and strengthen
> the core television narrative experience [...] for many people within the
> industry, trans-media is optimistically regarded as a magnet to sustain
> viewers' engagement and attention across these periodic gaps. (295)

If the final goal is to "always support and strengthen the core television
narrative experience," then it might be suggested that *Mad Men* appears to
be *too* good *in its own terms* for trans-media. Indeed, the AMC show achieves
the goal of keeping viewers engaged and interested because it offers a plot
and a set of characters that are considered challenging and multifaceted and,
hence, strategically intriguing. The additional material, ranging from the
quizzes to the fashion contests, is essentially perceived as an array of "killing
time" activities, which do not represent added value to the primary experience of watching and reflecting on the series' televisual content. But Mittell's
definition implies something more about trans-media as a media corporate
strategy, namely, the existence of a "*core* television narrative experience"
(Mittell 295; my emphasis). This notion poses questions about the creation of
trans-media structures that strictly adhere to the definition provided by Henry
Jenkins, according to which there are no hierarchies among texts—therefore,
among experiences—in trans-media, since each text is meant to contribute
something new to the expansion of the fictional world. In Jenkins's understanding, all texts are weighted equally in offering meaningful experiences of
the fictional story-world. This is the premise behind what can be considered
"balanced trans-media" (Mittell 292–94): each experience is a core one that
brings valuable knowledge about the imaginary universe. This being said,
when it comes to a series like *Mad Men*, it is undeniable that the viewing experience stands as the most important one, and all the other related practices
in which fans engage outside the timeframe of watching end up reinforcing
the relevance of this core activity because they keep bringing fans back to the
text. From this perspective, the concept of "unbalanced trans-media" (Mittell
292–94) seems more appropriate to describe the *Mad Men* expanded structure: the essential role played by the various media extensions in this show's
architecture is "to drive viewers back to the television series" (Mittell 295),
without necessarily contributing something new to how the program is experienced. But the specificity of the "*Mad Men* experience" goes beyond a relation

between text and para-texts in an unequal network of elements; rather, the series comes out as so challenging and fascinating that it becomes a magnet *in itself* for fans. The text fully covers the reconstruction of Don Draper's world, with its intriguing and relatable "madness," and serves as the source of the emotional experience that captures fans' interest and secures their loyalty, in a way that does not require further stimuli from quizzes, recipes, contests, games and collectibles. For *Mad Men*, this is where the strategy essentially lies: in its delicate, yet potent, capacity to create a sentimental bond with the audience through the stories, the characters and the themes of its representation, within the boundaries of that convoluted universe depicted on the screen(s).

GAME OF THRONES

BETWEEN FANTASY AND REALISM

One of the primary reasons that individuals watch movies and TV programs is the possibility of experiencing fictional realities in which they can feel emotionally immersed. *Game of Thrones'* narrative is characterized by elements that emphasize its fictitious world, since these elements belong to the fantasy genre, which, by definition, deals with the supernatural.[12] Outrageous acts occur in *Game of Thrones*, but spectators are aware that this universe is not real, since this is something that is constantly reiterated through visual signifiers like the settings, the characters' costumes and weapons, the supernatural creatures (like dragons) and the overall structure of the society. The fantasy genre is instrumental in providing fans with just enough distance from the violent events represented so as to not be overwhelmed by their brutality.

However, things are never that simple in George R. R. Martin's universe— and the televisual one as well. In identifying what he calls the fantastic genres—horror, fantasy, fairy tale and science fiction—the cognitive film theorist Torben Grodal relies on the notions of "changes, deviations, and novelty," and affirms that the fantastic is "interesting precisely because it violates universal common sense" (Grodal 98, 103). In this regard, a recurrence of violation can also turn into a recognizable pattern, unless the violation itself is unpredictably violated. Rikke Schubart employs this notion to assert that "this is precisely what *Game of Thrones* does: it uses the rules (patterns) of the fantastic, yet twists them in surprising ways to [...] combin[e] the unique with tradition" (Schubart 107). This means that, instead of following the genre

---

[12] Fantasy refers to "a genre traditionally set in a secondary world full of adventure, supernatural elements (such as magic, monsters, witches, and wizards), a hero's quest, or coming-of-age story, and, perhaps most importantly, a utopian spirit shared with the fairy tale" (Gjelsvik and Schubart 5).

rules, "*Game of Thrones* articulates a striking refusal of the hopeful mythologies of high epic fantasy" (Tasker and Steenberg 189) by focusing on the brutal, the extreme, and the overall injustice and chaos that permeate a society in which war and death appear to be inescapable. Through offering up this systematic subversion of the rules, the show manages to generate contradictory feelings in audiences, ranging from fervent appreciation to agonized discomfort. This set of emotions represents the possible range of audience response to a fictional text that is entirely built on the intertwining of situations filled with tension, drama and the predations of power. The text's final intent is precisely to become a source of continual excitement for its followers. In this chapter, the textual schematic of *Game of Thrones* is examined through focus group participants' emotional reactions to themes and events as reported in their own words. Such an approach is instrumental to illustrating the reasons for their passion for the show as well as the main concerns that arise during the viewing of this TV series.

When fantasy turns dark, there is not much room left for the neat and reassuring logic of chivalric codes—instead, more space is made available for what, with regard to *Game of Thrones*, has been defined in terms of "excruciating realism" (Schubart and Gjelsvik 6). The concurrent presence of elements that derive from different genres constitute the richness of the text's multiple narrative layers, and the often extremist representation of sex and violence enriches the world of the series beyond the standard features of the classic fantasy story. In addition to the production values that characterize the representation, the intricacy of its plot and the complexity of its protagonists' profiles, it is precisely this dialectic of fantasy and realism[13] that stands as something peculiar to the narrative of *Game of Thrones*—and the fantastic universe of the series, so filled with intertwined and sensational occurrences, can also function as an escape route from everyday life, as the focus group participants articulate:

- "*My life sucks sometimes,* Game of Thrones *displays a much more interesting and alternative reality!*" [NZ]
- "*The world of* Game of Thrones *is far away but relatable at the same time.*" [IT]
- "*It is a fantastic world presented in a realistic way.*" [NZ]
- "*One of the things that I really liked from reading it, and from watching it, is that it's exactly true to the era.*" [NZ]

This is where the fascination of both the literary saga and the HBO series lies: in the nuanced depictions of a world where good and evil are not easily

---

[13] In this context, the term "realism" is employed with reference to the explanations provided by fans of the series in relation to the specific attributes of the TV program.

demarcated into binary, Manichean categories. Eric J. Silverman states: "Just as the real world isn't truly divided into quickly identifiable heroes in white hats and villains in dark hats, Westeros is not easily divided into a simplistic dichotomy of positive heroes and villains. In reality, most people are similar to morally imperfect 'grey' characters" (Silverman 214). In the fictional frame of the story, events and characters exhibit realistic traits in terms of human profiles and motivations, mainly related to the development of dramatic events, the idea of change and characters' internal conflicts and external struggles. Once again, it is the show's ability to convey the complexity of human nature that generates interest and attraction:

– *"There isn't a character who is constantly good from the beginning until the end, and this makes the series very realistic."* [IT]
– *"For* Game of Thrones, *the characters that I hate keep me watching more than the characters that I like."* [NZ]

GAME OF THRONES' AMBIVALENT PLEASURES: ALL THE NUANCES OF THE HUMAN BEING

These "grey" individuals are capable of behaving in ways that cannot always be predicted; indeed, they manage to produce contrasting emotions. Fans tend to feel close to those characters who have the courage to show their vulnerability and admit their own fears as well as to those who possess strong personalities, manage to overcome difficulties and have the perseverance to never give up on their goals. The recognition of similar feelings allows to see characters as human, a fact that can also foster a process of identification. Tyrion Lannister, Arya Stark, Daenerys Targaryen and Jon Snow are examples of characters who invoke this type of attitude among the majority of viewers:

– "Game of Thrones *creates this strong empathy with the characters, it is not like any other TV series and I do watch many! But with* Game of Thrones *you develop a real feeling of affection for the single character; he/she becomes one of us."* [IT]
– *"The fact that we do identify with the characters in such absurd situations, it is something weird, particular."* [IT]

On the other hand, figures like Joffrey Baratheon, Cersei's incestuous first-born, and Ramsay Bolton, Lord Bolton's bastard son, are personifications of evil who engage in extreme sadistic behavior. They generate feelings of hatred and resentment because fans recognize in them all those elements that are regarded as barbaric and destructive of human life and, hence, are rejected as traits of one's own personality. These same characters manage to provide the show with a type of visual and emotional drama that relies on the representa-tion of the darkest side of human actions.

Both identification and rejection entail a process of self-reflexivity that involves fans' adoption of a critical approach to the narrative. In reconsidering personal beliefs and behaviors, the majority of participants admitted that the show makes them think, reflecting on what they would be able to do—or *not* to do—if they were to find themselves in similar situations and conditions as those confronted by the characters. Indeed, the tendency to question char-acter behaviors and traits of their personality becomes a form of psychological reflexivity that reinforces the fascination of *Game of Thrones* in fans' minds, thus helping to explain the level of emotional involvement that the series is capable of eliciting. Furthermore, both identification and rejection can coexist as psy-chological attitudes that fans might experience toward the same character, a fact that impacts on the relevance that any particular figure may assume in the story. Overall, characters become reflective surfaces of viewers' real lives:

– *"A TV series that manages to instill such a hatred towards specific characters, I think it means that it is capable to build them in a very effective way."* [IT]

Among the main protagonists Arya Stark, Cersei Lannister and Daenerys Targaryen present a significant character development that is also deeply con-troversial. The three female figures are of particular interest when it comes to considerations regarding spectators' reactions about gender representations. Tasker and Steenberg point out "Arya's liminal status" (184) as a condition that exemplifies the nature of *Game of Thrones*' world—a place populated by many "complex, border-crossing figures" (184), like the Wildlings, the White Walkers, the imp Tyrion Lannister and the eunuch Lord Varis. This notion of "liminality" (185) calls attention to both the intricacy of the series' protagonists and to the range of audience responses as a result of being presented with inherently ambiguous and unpredictable situations and characters. E. M. Dadlez analyzes the maturation of Ned Stark's youngest daughter from this perspective, and notes that Arya's vehement desire for revenge is made understandable (from her point of view) to the public while, at the same time, her capacity to perform violence and inflict pain escalates:

> The television series in particular arouses a revulsion intended to con-flict with our positive response to Arya's youth and courage [...] We are made to see how [the killings] can appear desirable from Arya's perspec-tive, but they are never endorsed—indeed, the reverse is often true, espe-cially in the case of the assassination of the individual whose culpability is never established. (Dadlez 10)

Participants' feelings toward this character also turned out to be of conflicting nature:

– *"I admire Arya because she has gone through so much!"* [NZ]
– *"The scene that made me think 'I do not want to go on watching this series!' is the one in which Arya kills a man in the last season [...] Too much cruelty! She used to be a defenseless little girl but now all this hate has come out [...] No, I do not want to watch that scene ever again!"* [IT]

On a similar note, the Machiavellian maneuvering of Queen Cersei,[14] her merciless acts of vengeance and contemptible behavior are always counterbalanced by the relevance given to her one redeeming quality—her unconditional love for her children as the main motivator of her actions (plus her cheekbones, according to her brother Tyrion): "Queen Cersei may be incestuous and vengeful, but she is also a devoted mother" (Gjelsvik and Schubart 6). This appears to be a fundamental trait when it comes to fans' considerations regarding the reasons that push Cersei to act in a specific way, to the point that it can outweigh the savagery of her deeds:

– *"Most of the time I absolutely hate Cersei, but then you realize that she loves her children so much, and you feel so sorry for this woman that you hated for five seasons."* [NZ]
– *"I love Cersei because she does everything for the love of her children and family; she is one of the best characters!"* [IT]

The evolution of Daenerys Targaryen—future *Khaleesi* and Mother of Dragons—incorporates narrative passages that pertain to both the fairy tale and the adventure genre, in a combination of pivotal tests and situations that comes out as a potent and suggestive storyline. In being depicted as the "female fantasy hero" of the show, Daenerys emerges as the expression of qualities that are generally used to define male attributes, like ambition, power, strength, determination. In being a woman, her character is made even more complex, for the transformation she is forced to undergo requires the realization of a sense of personal worth. From being a submissive, frightened young girl, Daenerys develops into a self-confident and wise woman, fully aware of the power she has progressively achieved but, nonetheless, capable of experiencing compassion and vulnerability. In learning how to master these

---

[14] Elizabeth Beaton analyses the attitude and behavior of Queen Cersei through the lens of Machiavellian politics. She asserts, "Cersei is a Machiavellian of the court, and she possesses a dignity that goes beyond clothing; a dignity of conduct that is manifest in her body language and actions" (Beaton 203).

emotions along a path filled with obstacles and suffering, the figure of Daenerys becomes a modern symbol of hope and positive advancement that would even be too simplistic to reduce to either feminist or postfeminist readings:

– *"I like Daenerys because she always manages to change the situation to her advantage […] I wish I were like her sometimes."* [IT]
– *"I like Daenerys for her ability to overturn situations!"* [IT]

From this perspective, *Game of Thrones* is seen as a progressive show because it promotes female figures that are empowered, responsible for their own choices and capable of pursuing their goals and of fighting for a legitimate place in a male-oriented society. Arya Stark, Cersei Lannister and Daenerys Targaryen are the main personifications of these driven personalities, and even if their acts put them in "dark places"—both physically and metaphorically, since they all end up perpetrating dreadful actions—their strength and determination exert an unquestionable fascination on the majority of fans:[15]

– *"There are many female characters that are so strong, and this is different from the standard fantasy story."* [NZ]
– *"I like the challenges in terms of gender representations, so many strong female characters!"* [NZ]

Nevertheless, due to the presence of visual and narrative elements that emphasize the exploitation and devaluation of women, *Game of Thrones* remains a site of conflict, a matter of open debate that—even if still unresolved—manages to draw our attention to the potent depiction of fully rounded, highly captivating and enigmatic characters: "Women in *Game of Thrones* are psychologically complex, sexually transgressive, ideologically ambiguous, and intimately grounded in human emotions" (Schubart and Gjelsvik 9).

The male counterparts of Arya and Daenerys are the figures of Jon Snow and Tyrion Lannister. Strong, brave, smart and perceptive, both Jon and Tyrion also exhibit vulnerable personalities. In being forced to live under

---

[15] *"Game of Thrones* also explores women's relationship to institutional power in a variety of ways—while acknowledging that whatever this relationship might be, it is always categorically gendered. […] *Game of Thrones* offers women who are emperors, slaves and everything in between. It is a world in which women who seem to be pawns have a way of turning out to be queens; but it is also a world that knows queens can always be taken." (Sarah Churchwell, "Drama Queens: Why It's All about Women and Power on Screen Right Now," *Guardian*, July 22, 2017, https://www.theguardian.com/books/2017/jul/22/game-of-thrones-handmaids-tale-wonder-woman-female-power (accessed July 26, 2017)).

problematic conditions—Jon as Ned Stark's bastard son, Tyrion as a dwarf, always ridiculed by others—they both symbolize the human state of having to struggle for acceptance. This condition contributes to the realism of the representation, and determines sentiments of compassion and empathy in fans, who tend to feel closer to those who have to continually fight the judgment of society. In particular, the way Tyrion employs irony to react to other characters' comments and attacks, as well as to point out the absurdity or unfairness of certain situations, helps him gain viewers' sympathy. In turn, viewers tend to see in him a little man with a high sense of morality, capable of speaking the truth: "[Tyrion] has the capability to point out the ridiculousness of other people's thought patterns, and he's not afraid to share his observations. Thanks to his wit, Tyrion's exceptional mind is on display" (Hietalahti 28).

Out of this intricate texture of attitudes and emotions, *Game of Thrones* builds a dynamic tension between the desire/curiosity to watch what is compelling but often almost unsustainable, and the refusal of excessively violent images. In this way, the series manages to offer its viewers a spectacle of horrors and excitement with the final intent to foster ambivalent forms of pleasure, overtly high in adrenaline content and ingeniously provocative. Stephanie Genz investigates the concept of the "guilty-pleasure" spectacle as a way of answering "why the series has captured our imagination to such an extent" (Genz 243). Genz explicitly asserts: "Undeniably, because of the raunchy and explicit content, one explanation can be found in audiences' *voyeuristic viewing pleasures* as they delight in the spectacle of violence and sex" (243; my emphasis). Watching *Game of Thrones* can, indeed, amount to an exceptionally intense, even disruptive, experience, in particular with reference to the representation of both sex and violence.

Sex, in particular, is depicted as a form of spectacle—ranging from flirtation, carnal intercourses and romantic relations to lesbian performances, sexual titillation, orgies and rape[16]—that can be either demeaning or empowering. This elicits contrasting responses among the show's followers:

– *"Come for the sex, stay for the politics!"* [NZ]
– *"I'll say only this: there are boobs, fights and dragons… What else do we need?!"* [IT]

---

[16] But why no gay sex in *Game of Thrones*? It appears to be a legitimate question to ask. On this matter, George Martin stated that a TV show does not have to have specific limitations, subtly implying that anything might still happen. Furthermore, the novelist also revealed that, according to the fans' letters he has been receiving, some of them would like to see explicit male sex scenes in *Game of Thrones*. Interestingly enough, most of the times these postulants are women: https://www.theguardian.com/books/2014/aug/11/george-rr-martin-game-of-thrones-gay-sex (accessed July 14, 2017).

– *"I just find the nudity a bit too much, sometimes."* [NZ]
– *"I can't stand Sansa, they did the right thing to have her raped!"* [IT]

Some of the series' most explicit scenes and sequences have also inspired pornographic versions of the storylines, and have scored significant views on the popular website PornHub, where scenes from the show, as well as parodies, have been distributed. In 2016, HBO decided to sue PornHub for copyright infringement in order to force the removal of the content from the website. It is worth noting that, during the broadcasting of the sixth season of the show, viewing figures related to PornHub "dropped dramatically," whereas just few days before the series' premiere "searches for *Game of Thrones* related porn increased exponentially."[17] It is indisputable that the series generates a *peculiar* interest in those elements of the plot that focus on sex and its, often extreme, representations. The comments and the conversations regarding the pornographic nature of *Game of Thrones* call attention to the interest and curiosity that the show manages to provoke, as well as to the limits—in terms of what is permissible and watchable on screen—that the series tends to challenge.

Violence as depicted in the TV program traumatizes the audience by presenting a world of terror and atrocities that does not hold back anything in terms of brutal acts. This aspect becomes, once again, the source of contrasting attitudes among the audience: it generates both attraction and repulsion. In this regard, some fans expressed their acceptance of all the terrible acts and events that take place in *Game of Thrones*, since, for them, they feel justified by the realistic representation of a society that resembles the Middle Age. During those times, rape, murder and torture were essential attributes of society.[18] At the core of this debate about the "excessive" realism of *Game of Thrones*, George Martin's words help to situate his approach to the significance of sex and violence in the construction of his fictional universe:

> rape and sexual violence have been a part of every war ever fought, from the ancient Sumerians to our present day. To omit them from a narrative centered on war and power would have been fundamentally false and dishonest, and would have undermined one of the themes

---

[17] See also http://www.telegraph.co.uk/tv/2016/06/01/hbo-sues-pornhub-over-game-of-thrones-copyright/ (accessed July 14, 2017); http://www.digitalspy.com/tv/game-of-thrones/news/a795922/game-of-thrones-hbo-pornhub-copyright-issue/ (accessed July 14, 2017); https://broadly.vice.com/en_us/article/ae55wg/this-is-how-much-porn-traffic-dropped-during-the-game-of-thrones-season-finale (accessed July 14, 2017).

[18] See also Itzkoff.

of the books: that the true horrors of human history derive not from orcs and Dark Lords, but from ourselves. We are the monsters (and the heroes too). (Flood)

In this sense, the depiction of violence appears to be instrumental to re-creating the illusion of reality as well as to increasing the spectacularity of the show:

– *"In* Game of Thrones *violence is a matter of realism and it also contributes to the development of the characters."* [NZ]
– *"*Game of Thrones *is realistic, and this means that the representation of violence is necessary because in the Middle Age people did not behave in such a different way."* [IT]

On the other hand, other fans revealed a resentful attitude toward scenes and sequences regarded as too extreme in the way violence is portrayed on the screen, hence quite disturbing and disconcerting. For these fans, the violence in *Game of Thrones* turned out to be a source of profound discomfort that can produce a reaction of recoil and even rejection. In between attraction and repulsion, a middle-ground position belongs to those fans who explicitly stated that they are at the same time intrigued and appalled by the representation of violence:

– *"Every season people say that they will stop watching it but it doesn't actually happen."* [NZ]
– *"There are specific scenes/sequences that make you think: 'This is actually too much, I am going to stop watching it now,' but you know that you won't do it. You will keep going back to it."* [NZ]

Violence in *Game of Thrones* emerges as fundamentally controversial also in terms of moral rewards and formal punishments. In fact, given the controversial nature of the acts that form the central battles over power and the complex motivations behind characters' behaviors, a clear, indisputable distinction between what constitutes "justice" and what constitutes "revenge" emerges as highly debatable. The moral code in the universe of *Game of Thrones* is inherently ambiguous, and for a valid reason. The objective is to allow viewers to have feelings that can amount to ambivalent forms of gratification and disgust, especially when the characters' storylines include moments that are symptomatic of a new pattern in the dynamics of power. Each single character in *Game of Thrones* can be, at different times and from different perspectives, a victim or an executioner:[19] to classify one's acts as a

---

[19] In the world of *Game of Thrones*, what stands as apparent is a sort of "inversion of the Tolkienian consolation" (Johnston 141).

form of "justice" or "revenge" is essentially a matter of how the character's motivations, at that specific point in the story, are perceived by viewers. What is worth noting is audiences' fluctuating attitude in picking sides, in condemning or justifying characters' actions. This dynamic becomes the basis on which the show constructs its suspense and narrative twists; it is highly involving for fans, who appreciate the unpredictability of the plot and the possibility of experiencing a diverse set of emotions toward characters who are capable of any kind of deeds:

> – *There is no "deus ex machina," at least not just one [...] There is no such a thing as a predictable happy ending just for the sake of it!* [NZ]
> – *The truth is that we are surprised when things go fine [...] We expect the twists, and we enjoy it a lot more when things start to go wrong!* [IT]

But when it comes to the visual combination of violence and explicit sex, some of the show's representations turn out to be very problematic.[20] According to critics and reviewers, the series has already gone too far, pushing the limits of what is considered admissible on the screen. In particular, specific events in the intertwined stories of Jaime and Cersei Lannister, Ramsay Bolton, Theon Greyjoy and Sansa Stark have provoked discussions and reactions that indicate both indignation and frustration. The issues at stake appear to be related to the inconsistency and/or the gratuitousness of events that, in the first place, are not justified by their presence in the original source of the series (Martin's books).[21] One such scene is Cersei's rape in the episode "Breaker of Chains" (S04E03), which has provoked heated debate and general criticism among reviewers, and even irritation among fans. Up until that point, Jaime was the kind of "bad-at-the-same-time-good" character that fans had gradually learned to like, in part because redemption[22] had been foreshadowed as an achievable condition for him. The sexual assault of his sister by the coffin of their dead son Joffrey repositioned Jaime as a sordid character without any

---

[20] "Representations that combine sex and violence—that, for instance, depict rape—are located on a disconcerting threshold between discursive reality and fictional discourse" (Larsson 18).

[21] "HBO has been accused of shoehorning sex scenes into the *Game of Thrones'* storyline, and critics have debated whether the showrunners David Benioff and D. B. Weiss are 'rewriting the books into misogyny,' in particular, by adding sexually explicit scenes that are neither in the books, nor of vital importance to the storyline" (Gjelsvik 58).

[22] The heinous act that Jaime has been hated for since the beginning of *Game of Thrones* is the attempt to kill Bran, Ned Stark's child, in order to protect his incestuous relationship with his twin sister Cersei.

apparent justification[23] and generated controversy among followers. On the one hand, shocking events demand a meticulous process of build-up within the characters' lines of development in order to be fully comprehended and accepted. This something that is expected (even) by the fans of *Game of Thrones*, who appear to be willing to accept (almost) everything if they can recognize, and understand, the function of that specific element as part of the story:

– *"The fact that* Game of Thrones *shows that much violence and sex is something that we actually like* **because it appears to be instrumental to the story**.*"* [my emphasis, NZ]

Seemingly, this was not the case with Jaime's aggression.[24] On the other hand, rape—especially when it comes to visual media—is always a problem.

Film scholar Margrethe Bruun Vaage has conducted studies on the morally questionable behaviors of characters in TV shows such as *Dexter, The Sopranos* and *The Wire*, and she came to the conclusion that, no matter how ferocious their actions might be, their limit is always clear: these individuals do not rape, as "contemporary television viewers will ally with mobsters, murderers, and serial killers, but not with rapists" (Gjelsvik 61). Essentially, the problem with showing rape—instead of, for instance, reading about it—has been pointed out by Tom Gunning in the following terms: "We do not just *see* motion and we are not simply affected emotionally by its role within a plot; we *feel* it in our guts or throughout our bodies" (Gunning 261). Anne Gjelsvik employs Gunning's definition to further explain:

> Violence toward the human body, and in particular sexual violence, often feels more intimate when seen than read. In addition, sexual violence is a more common experience among viewers than, for instance, battles and sword fighting, and is, therefore, more likely to elicit stronger emotional reactions. (Gjelsvik 70)

---

[23] One reviewer referred to this scene in "Breaker of Chains" (S04E03) as "the most screwed up sex scene ever broadcast on television." (Stern).

[24] With regard to this scene, George Martin himself felt the urgency to apologize because the sexual intercourse was clearly shown in the series as an act of rape, whereas in the book the sex is described as consensual. Nonetheless, Anne Gjelsvik observes that

> Jaime suffers no consequences for the rape. [...] An interesting explanation for this, based on different interviews, is that both producers and director did not intend it to be rape. However, this leads to an even more depressing hypothesis: namely, that HBO's production team didn't know what it was doing and, thus, was unaware of the consequences of their choice. (Gjelsvik 64)

When sex is utilized as a means of systematic degradation, one possible result is that what is shown on the screen is perceived as *too realistic* in terms of brutality and abusiveness, to the point that those who watch are both attracted to and horrified by the things they can see.[25]

These considerations help to understand the feelings of disgust and insane curiosity that emerge in response to the (alleged) gratuitousness of scenes that manage to destabilize viewers in ways that become always more and more extreme. Ramsay Bolton's ferocious deeds seem to validate the allegations that *Game of Thrones* is, basically, torture porn.[26] The castration of Theon Greyjoy at the climax of an endless (for Theon, especially!) period of indescribable torture as well as the rape of Sansa Stark on the night of her wedding with Ramsay mark the threshold of a new territory from the perspective of the visualization of sex and violence in the series: "While violence is something disturbing that happens to the characters in Martin's fictional world, its sexualization on television has become something disturbing that might interfere with the audience's willingness to be transported to Westeros" (Gjelsvik 71). Not everybody is willing to follow along with this graphic turn:

– *"In terms of Sansa getting raped, I think that that was just shock-value, I didn't like it, because I thought that the director was just trying to generate controversy for controversy sake, especially because it was not in the books."* [NZ]

---

[25] Zoe Williams in the *Guardian* writes about the show's capacity to generate ambivalent forms of pleasures—and the *real* reason why people like *Game of Thrones*:

> But I think the uniqueness is that, following the plot of the George RR Martin's books, it doesn't have any of the cynicism of television. TV writing can be magnificent, as good as any writing has ever been. But it's also instrumental. You would never kill Sean Bean in a TV script. You might want to, but when it came to it, you would just say he's too good. You would never have a red wedding, and let your carefully tended family, that you'd built and differentiated and intertwined in beautiful ways, die all at once. You would arrange the cast so that there weren't too many big hitters in a scene. And those rules are really good, but they also lose something, some property of unpredictability, some cruelty to the audience, that is the real uniqueness of Game of Thrones. *It doesn't just disregard you, viewer: it despises you. And that's what you love about it.*" (Williams; my emphasis).

[26] Madeleine Davis on Theon's emasculation: "It's not uncommon that *Game of Thrones* gets accused of being torture porn—senseless, objectifying violence combined with senseless, objectifying sexual imagery—but it is rare that I can wholeheartedly agree that it *is* torture porn […] This week, however, the show managed to teeter over the line that they've drawn themselves and fall onto the wrong side" (Davies).

In the game for the conquest of the Iron Throne, an immeasurable thirst for power and the numerous conspiracies fill out the drama. Fans relate these elements to the concept of politics in *Game of Thrones*. The development of the political theme in the series is usually explained through the logic that pertains to the political treatise *The Prince* (1532) by Niccolò Machiavelli. In his famous masterpiece, Machiavelli adopts a pragmatic approach to deduce the best qualities that a generic ruler—called "the Prince"—must have in order to govern a state. In particular, this individual must possess the ability to employ deception, as well as to exert both strength and violence in order to maintain stability and preserve power. Ruled by ferocious warmongers, populated by devious advisors and concealed assassins, the world of *Game of Thrones* retains a close resemblance with the society presented by Machiavelli in the treatise, characterized by military crises and political intrigue. Indeed, Elizabeth Beaton notes that George R. R. Martin's "efforts to capture human behaviour and experience involve returning again and again to Machiavellian antics [...] his narratives [...] suggest that pragmatic politics are at the heart of a captivating human story" (198). Furthermore, in an interview in Melbourne in late 2013 with Beaton, Martin admitted the influence of Machiavelli on his work by saying: "His advice in *The Prince* is one way to approach rule." (Elizabeth Beaton, interview with George R. R. Martin (Melbourne, November 14, 2013)). In addition to this, in another interview, the novelist described Petyr Baelish as "one of the most Machiavellian characters" in the series (Alan Yentob, interview with George Martin, November 26, 2013).

The convoluted network of constant backstabbing, unpredictable alliances, manipulative actions and lies that propels the story forward and permeates the show's storylines with suspense mirrors many of the situations described by Machiavelli as to specific tactics that are to be employed in order to perpetuate, or realize, political dominance and obedience. Nonetheless, even if the "game of politics" is mainly played by male figures at different levels of the social ladder (e.g., Petyr Baelish and Lord Varis), female characters like Cersei and Daenerys are also presented as active participants in this strategic scheming filled with "Machiavellian moments": "when taking risks and exposing themselves to danger, Martin's women gain strength and demonstrate their political agency with practical maneuvers" (Beaton 193). In the patriarchal political system that structures the society of *Game of Thrones*, these moments that display female tenacity and determination appear to be well appreciated by the show's followers. Indeed, Eliana Dockterman stated that "the show is strongest when it has 'scenes of female empowerment' to provide balance with scenes in which women are oppressed" (209). In this regard, Elizabeth Beaton goes even further by asserting that "the triumphs and bold maneuvers of exceptional women within a ruthless, patriarchal world provide a kind of feminist pleasure" (211).

All these elements appeal to the audience because the TV program emerges as a combination of genres capable of satisfying different types of viewers— from those who like the supernatural and the magical, or those who enjoy the intense action, to those who are more passionate about the drama and the intrigues. Even the titillating nature of the series' representation becomes a source of "guilty pleasure" that provokes viewers all the while it upsets them:

– *"I think that the show is really controversial, and that's why people like it. It's kind of like 'guilty pleasure', there's a lot of blood and sex."* [NZ]

According to Shannon Wells-Lassagne, George Martin's universe "has contributed to the creation of a new and dark fantasy genre where Middle Earth takes on a decidedly more gritty feel." (Wells-Lassagne 39). In showing the dark side of the fantasy genre, in turning violence into a source of perverse excitement while also showing intense moments of human compassion and long-awaited justice, *Game of Thrones* has succeeded in transcending the boundaries of a simple categorization. This is readily recognized by fans as a major positive quality of the series:

– *"The series has the right mix of love, hate and power."* [IT]
– "Game of Thrones *is not just action, you also have the drama and the tension; it is worth the wait for everything!"* [NZ]
– *"The series knows how to touch your emotions. You find this whole new world in front of you and you feel like you are in it. It is really engaging and fascinating, no other series is like* Game of Thrones *at the moment!"* [IT]

OFFICIAL TRANS-MEDIA STRUCTURE OF GAME OF THRONES

The basic idea that underlies the serialized narrative of *Game of Thrones* is that of the game: characters are continually involved in dangerous confrontations and strategic fights for the sake of conquest and power. The series' fictional framework has been conceived accordingly. The main features, apps[27] and board games available online and on mobile devices are structured like interactive games for the purpose of involving audiences in a system of competitions

---

[27] *Game of Thrones* applications for iPhones and smartphones are numerous. For instance: "Game of Thrones Companion," "Game of Thrones Wiki," "Game of Thrones Trivia With Friends," "A Game of Thrones Reference," "News for GoT," "IQuiz For Game of Thrones," "Ice & Fire."

that reinforce the brand image of the product. The "world-building experience"[28] (Gambarato 4) is possible thanks to the employment of the core concepts of trans-media storytelling inside the structure of the shows. The universe of *Game of Thrones* presents multiple entry points, via different media technologies, and this circuit of extensive content allows followers to actively engage in a process of information exchange and re-elaboration of the events and stories, through which they may also be able to detect gaps and excesses in the narrative. The aim is to keep viewers updated on what is new about the production of the TV show, allowing each fan to engage in games with friends and to test their own knowledge of the universe created by George R. R. Martin.

The HBO official website of *Game of Thrones* (http://www.hbo.com/game-of-thrones) consists of trailers, previews, an official viewer's guide and a wide collection of videos that includes recaps from the previous seasons, interviews with the cast and crew, and behind-the-scenes clips.[29] Furthermore, HBO has launched HBO GO, a geo-specific application for Android and Apple devices through which is possible to watch the series episodes at any moment during the day, as well as HBO NOW, a new standalone streaming service that requires an Internet subscription to watch the series, movies, documentaries and sports events that are part of HBO programming. HBO GO and HBO NOW represent one of the most important media strategies adopted by the network, since the ultimate aim is to saturate viewers' time with a product available anytime, anywhere. For instance, the video "The Game Revealed Takes You Behind the Scenes" provides fans with the "making of" footage from several episodes in Season 6, and is advertised on the official website as available for streaming on the HBO NOW application. In the "About the Show" area of the website one can find a general presentation of *Game of Thrones*' plot under *Series Information* together with the *Related Media* content, although the former is only partly accessible to people who are outside of North America. In "Cast & Crew," a detailed list of characters' bios is enriched by a series of videos, called *Character Feature*, which present interviews with the actors/actresses together with scenes from the show. The "Episodes" section presents a collection of all the episodes from the first season to the sixth, and for each episode there is a comprehensive synopsis plus other content, which usually includes an inside-the-episode video, a preview, interviews with the cast and an assemblage of photos. All

---

[28] For a more detailed description of the concept of "world-building", see Wolf.
  On this topic, see also http://henryjenkins.org/2013/09/building-imaginary-worlds-an-interview-with-mark-j-p-wolf-part-one.html (accessed July 14, 2017).
[29] The following description refers to the organization of the website at the time of writing.

this material is accessible to all fans, whereas for the actual viewing of the full episodes the basic conditions require a subscription to HBO and by the fact that is necessary to be in the United States.

Visitors are treated not only to an overview, but also to "special" information. The "Inside" segment, for instance, contains interviews with the show's main protagonists; the *Inside the Episode* collection offers a selection of short videos in which show-runners David Benioff and D. B. Wise comment on the main events of a single episode; and the *Extras* area is composed of an assortment of elements that go beyond the basic informative function. Indeed, the combination of links, features, applications, items and games are instrumental to stimulate fans' involvement with the show by offering updates on the development of the plot (newsletter, HBO's *Making* Game of Thrones), virtual places for discussions (Facebook, Twitter, HBO Connect), means for interaction and creativity (Screensaver, Avatars, Join the Realm, Tumblr) and design prints (Desktop Wallpapers, House Wallpapers, iPhone House Wallpapers, Quote Wallpapers). From the HBO shop potential buyers can choose among books, dolls, figurines, accessories, mugs and glasses, posters and maps, T-shirts, cards, lunchboxes, exercise books, bookends, paperweights and magnet sets. The opportunity that the show gives fans to investigate the content in depth is defined in terms of "drillability": "a vertical descent into a text's complexities" implies "immersion" (Gambarato 6) into the fictional universe generated by the story. The array of sections, applications, games, interactive features and online discussions are all means to this end. In addition, the concept of "extractability" "refers to the possibility fans may have to appropriate aspects of the story (e.g., purchase of memorabilia)" (6), as *Game of Thrones'* extensive merchandise options show.

On the home page of the HBO website, further sections that allow fans to acquire a more comprehensive insight into the *Game of Thrones'* universe as well as to feel part of it include sections called Explore More on "Making *Game of Thrones*," Experience the Opening Titles Like Never Before, and Join the Hall of Faces.[30] The first section is varied and rich in its organization

---

[30] The "Hall of Faces" houses skinned faces of the dead, and is found in a great hall within the House of Black and White. The "Hall of Faces" lies within a large, secret chamber. It is made of stone, with many pillars that are recipients for all the faces of the dead. Indeed, cleansed faces of corpses are skinned and hung to dry within this place. The Faceless Men use the combination of magic spells and faces of the dead to create their different camouflages. It is Jaqen H'ghar the faceless man, the one who brings Arya to the Hall of Faces where she works as an acolyte in order to learn how to become "No One." For a full explanation of the structure and the function of the "Hall of Faces," see http://gameofthrones.wikia.com/wiki/Hall_of_Faces and http://gameofthrones.wikia.com/wiki/House_of_Black_and_White.

since it incorporates a written interview with the *Game of Thrones*' music composer Ramin Djawadi ("Ramin Djawadi Shares Secrets of GoT Composing, Characters and Concerts"); a quiz on the music employed in the series ("See How Well You Know the Music of *Game of Thrones*"); two informative segments ("Everything There Is to Know about *Game of Thrones* Season 7" and "Lena Headey, *GoT* Receive Golden Globe Nominations"); a presentation of a behind-the-scenes experience that took place in different North American cities (like Los Angeles and Chicago) in celebration of the release of *Game of Thrones* Season 6 on DVD and Blu-ray ("Immerse Yourself in a GoT behind-the-Scenes Experience"), a guide to fancy gifts from the HBO online shop ("Your Ultimate Game of Thrones Holiday Gift Guide"); a list of purchasable items to embellish the house ("Suit-Up in *Game of Thrones*' Finest This Halloween"); and a presentation of the most prestigious TV awards from 2016 ("*Game of Thrones*' Triumphs at 2016 Emmys"). The second section has been conceived as "an immersive 360 experience" that exalts the already spectacular three-dimensional nature of the opening scene. The last one allows a more involved participation, since it offers fans the possibility to become "No One" by uploading a personal photo on the site and then starting a journey along the Hall of Faces.

It is important to keep in mind that "multimedia, cross-media and trans-media are points on a fluid spectrum that blend from one to the next" (Moloney). The definitions of these categories are themselves debatable; nonetheless, some media content dwells on the border of what can be strictly classified as multi-, cross- or trans-media, since it creates the conditions for a deeper engagement with the show in forms that do not strictly extend the narrative world. This is, for instance, the case with "*Game of Thrones* Pinterest," an official social media offshoot of the show where it is possible to find a variety of Westerosi fashions, recipes, quotes and similar content. While this may loosely be termed a cross-media extension, other games, interactive features and applications represent examples of trans-media extensions since they provide fans with the possibility to interact with each other, produce creative pieces of work and explore the series' world more in depth, so as to discover new elements that enrich its narrative. In this regard, HBO has created "*Game of Thrones*: Join the Realm," which allows fans to pick their own house, customize their own sigil and, through the Twitter hashtag #JoinTheRealm, share their creations with other fans. On "*Game of Thrones* Tumblr," fans can express their personal creativity and see a wide collection of fan art pieces from their favorite series on the multimedia content platform. In addition to the games offered by the official producers, "*Game of Thrones* Ascent" is a videogame developed by Disruptor Beam that was awarded Facebook Game of the Year 2013; the game allows players to become a noble during the era described both in the books and the series, so that players can unite both story and strategy by entering the world of Westeros. *"Game of Thrones*: The Game" is a role-playing game produced by Focus Home Interactive for PC, Xbox and Playstation 3. The game offers players an immersive experience, in that they can travel to various locations from the series and even meet with famous characters.

An even more involving but also limited experience for all the fans who have the desire to enter the world of Westeros is the Live Concert Experience named "Music Is Coming," which promises to "use innovative music tour production and video technology to recreate the various kingdoms found throughout Westeros and Essos, showcasing Game of Thrones footage and new imagery created for the tour" (http://www.makinggameofthrones.com/production-diary/got-live-concert-experience).[31] The live event, entirely based in the United States across 28 cities, restricts the experience to those fans who have the opportunity to be physically present on site during the course of the tour. This aspect is significant because it underlines the relevance of geographical position to the concrete possibility of taking part in an array of experiences that, overall, have been redefining the concept of audience engagement with media products. Indeed, in addition to the impossibility of watching the core content (the full episodes) on the official website outside of the United States[32] for reasons related to the policy adopted by HBO, the limitation of initiatives such as live concerts and exhibitions to the country of origin further narrows the effectiveness of place-based trans-media strategies in creating involving experiences for fans at an international level. This element turns out to be substantial since it emerges from the focus group findings—especially those of the Italian fans—as a particular form of cultural perception of one society by another, and highlights the relevance that this different treatment appears to have on what people decide to consume and how they become invested in foreign cultural products.

GAME OF THRONES' "CENTRIFUGAL COMPLEXITY": THE SERIES AS A VEHICLE FOR SOCIAL INTERACTION

"Centrifugal complexity" is a concept introduced by Jason Mittell that can be employed to describe the narrative of *Game of Thrones*. As already noted, this

---

[31] Accessed July 14, 2017.

[32] In this sense, a further example is given by the "*We're sorry. This video is not available in your region*" caption with regard to the "Watch 'Winter Is Coming' for Free" section on the home page of the HBO website, and that immediately catches the attention of people who access the site from outside the United States.

type of complexity refers to a story "in which the ongoing narrative pushes outward, spreading characters across an expanding story-world. On a centrifugal program, there is no single narrative center, as the action traces what happens between characters and institutions as they spread outward. It is not just that the series expands in quantity of characters and settings but that its richness is found in the complex web of interconnectivity forged across the social system rather than in the depth of any one individual's role in the narrative or psychological layers" (222–23). The vastness and complexity of the *Game of Thrones* reality—with its multiple spatial centers, intertwined events and a diverse array of characters that prove a challenge for fans to memorize due to the intricacy of their relationships—outline a fictional universe so rich in the mixture of its storylines and characters' profiles that fans feel the need to confront each other with the possible ramifications of the plot. As a matter of fact, the creation of an imaginary cosmos whose internal richness is constructed on both written and visual material (the Martin's novels and the HBO TV program), provided with a significant quantity of detail, becomes a concrete opportunity for fans to exchange thoughts and personal opinions about the overall development of events and storylines. Fans stated that they tend to use different technological devices to comment on the show (i.e., WhatsApp messages, message texts, phone conversations):

– *"My sister, some friends and I have created a WhatsApp group and we use it to share comments on the episodes."* [IT]
– *"Sometimes, when something dramatic happens, I text a friend to comment on what I have just seen, like: 'Oh, My God, someone just died!'"* [NZ]
– *"I do comment during the viewing on Twitter."* [IT]
– *"I discuss it a lot with my friends, face to face and over the phone."* [IT]
– *"Regardless of the shared viewing, we always comment on the episode via means of communication."* [IT]
– *"When we watch the episodes, we comment on what is happening."* [NZ]

Face-to-face conversations with friends and/or close relatives are highly regarded by fans, since they also represent an opportunity for commenting on their personal reactions to the fictional events. From this perspective, these discussions become an essential part of the interpretive process that fans activate after the viewing:

– *"To discuss it with friends is the most important thing."* [IT]
– *"I usually watch the episodes by myself on the computer and then I comment with my friends the following day."* [IT]
– *"I talk about the episodes with my friends at school."* [NZ]

– *"I always go on the Facebook page of* Game of Thrones *to read about different opinions, and on Tumblr, and I talk about the episodes with my friends."* [NZ]

Much time is spent in proposing theories about the series, and in putting together hints and pieces from George R. R. Martin's narrative on the basis of which fans attempt to draw conclusions. In doing so, fans tend to reinforce their own sense of community. Indeed, the ideal movement of fan engagement, which goes in an opposite direction from that indicated by *Mad Men*, suggests that *Game of Thrones* pushes its fans to transcend the text, to move away from constantly returning to a core text, and toward a process made up of reflexive practices that focus on the text's narrative traits. To fully appreciate the complexity of the series, *Game of Thrones* is meant to be approached as an experience that, in addition to the viewing, comprises activities that help to construct a "web of interconnectivity" among fans. The waiting time for the new seasons is made more suspenseful and exciting by the fact that fans share and debate their theories. More than half of the participants admitted that they read reviews of the series' episodes and online comments, mainly on Facebook, Twitter, Instagram, Reddit, Tumblr. The final goal is to stay up to date with the direction in which the discussions about the show have been developing:

– *"After each episode, I read fans' comments online but I do not actively participate, I post some comments on my personal Facebook page sometimes."* [NZ]
– *"I read the comments on the social media and I also read about the theories, on Tumblr sometimes."* [NZ]
– *"On Reddit there's a lot about the theories and it is exciting to read them."* [NZ]
– *"There are various pages and groups of reference for* Game of Thrones *on Facebook."* [IT]
– *"It is like being part of a big group, especially when we exchange comments and when we play."* [IT]
– *"Yes, indeed! I also comment with people I don't know on Twitter."* [IT]
– *"I don't really actively look for any additional* Game of Thrones*' content, but if it pops up on social media I might click on it."* [NZ]

This intellectual work of clarification and predictions builds up great expectations, with the result that fans become more and more eager to figure out if they are correct about what they have envisioned—that is, if events will unfold in the same way they anticipated them. Nevertheless, when it comes to social media as the public arena where theories are proposed and discussed and reactions are scrutinized, fans revealed that these virtual sites can also develop into problematic "minefields."

Game of Thrones is a series full of twists and cliffhangers that hook viewers and incite them to keep watching in order to discover what is going to happen. These elements of the narrative tend to encourage an uninterrupted viewing process and usually represent the center of fans' conversations, both online and offline. For this reason, the "spoiler issue" is one of the main sources of concern for fans. Managing its effects becomes of great significance for them, since it impacts on the mode of viewing and generates distinct attitudes in approaching social media in order to participate in online discussions. The verification of the information that is disseminated, the ability to detect discussions that contain spoilers as well as the ability to post spoilers when they are least expected are all modes of communication that fuel the exchange dynamics of the community, and make fans aware of the rules that govern these forms of interaction. As a general tendency, fans respect the online etiquette that prevents people from "spoilering," unless they give a clear warning that they are about to do so:

– *"People online are pretty good about respecting other people who do not want spoilers."* [NZ]
– *"Yeah, I feel like there is the way to get away with them more than other shows."* [NZ]

However, the most effective way fans have to secure themselves against spoilers, and at the same time be part of the discussions, is to be up to date with the viewing schedule. In this regard, the practice of binge-watching is extremely useful to retrieve past episodes in order to catch up with the new seasons:

– *"The episodes are good to binge-watch because they have a continuous plot, so it's kind of easy to just press 'Next' rather than just stopping."* [NZ]
– *"The show's episodes always end with cliffhangers, so you always want to know what is going to happen!"* [NZ]

During the moderation of the focus groups, some fans declared their repudiation of spoilers that stand as an unwanted, undesired form of insight. For these fans—who *do* want to get the best out of the viewing of each episode—spoilers are brutal and must be avoided, because they ruin the enjoyment peculiar to the experience of awe and surprise determined by the unforeseen:[33]

– *"Spoilers are one of the reason why I started reading the books."* [NZ]
– *"I can't stand spoilers, they ruin everything!"* [NZ]

---

[33] Some fans particularly complained about the spoilers that anticipated the events at the centre of the "Red Weeding" episode in Season 3 one of the most shocking representations in the series so far.

- *"I hate spoilers!"* [NZ]
- *"I would not like spoilers at all! I got the Red Wedding spoiled for me and it would have been so good to experience it but I knew what it was going to happen […] No, I do not like spoilers."* [NZ]
- *"I would stop reading online comments the moment I realize that they have spoilers."* [NZ]

Other fans, instead, claimed that spoilers do not impact on the pleasure of their viewing. For them, obtaining knowledge about future events through spoilers does not constitute a limitation to the entertainment that the viewing of *Game of Thrones* can still ensure:

- *"I do not mind spoilers that much, I would keep watching the episodes."* [NZ]
- *"If it gets spoiled it kind of sucks but it wouldn't devastate me!"* [NZ]
- *"I do not care about the spoilers because I am also a reader of the books."* [IT]
- *"There are heaps of book readers that will spoiler everything on Facebook! I remember someone telling everybody that Oberyn was going to die but it is not a big deal to me."* [NZ]

From the same standpoint, there were fans who admitted that knowing a plot outcome is more important than avoiding spoilers. Therefore, they choose to purposely look for specific information on the development of the story and, even with spoilers, they still find several aspects of the series' narrative to focus on and enjoy:

- *"I am super impatient and I do want to know what happens next so, even with spoilers, even if I know what is going to happen, it does not impact the fact that I can still enjoy the viewing! I still get shocked, because there are many things you can focus on when you watch* Game of Thrones.*"* [NZ]
- *"I do not care about spoilers, I just don't mind because I can't wait to know!"* [NZ]

In between those who refuse spoilers and those who can tolerate them without being annoyed, there is a "middle ground" on which it is possible to position those fans who see spoilers as a valuable and appealing source of information, if delivered in the right way. Spoilers can be instrumental in promoting an atmosphere of suspense when, for instance, they are expressed in the form of subtle clues. This fact can intensify the feelings of expectation among fans:

- *"Sometimes, general spoilers build a lot of anticipation, like: 'Someone big is going to die in season five!,' but a major and specific one might be very annoying and then you cannot watch the episode in the same way."* [NZ]

But a sense of discomfort can still persist if the information is given in a too detailed and specific fashion. Indeed, as mentioned before, fans who do not want to be provided with specific revelations on the events to come tend to express their dissatisfaction toward those who ignore the online etiquette and post spoilers for their personal amusement. The dissemination of spoilers with the clear intent to ruin the moments of surprise for other fans constitutes a particular form of pleasure, one that suggests a form of gratification deeply connected to the use of a superior knowledge:

– *"I enjoy 'spoilering' for other people!"* [IT]
– *"Yes, it's the same for me!"* [IT]
– *"I watch the episodes on SKY with my mother as soon as they are aired because I can't wait to see them, and also because I do want to be the one who gives the spoilers."* [IT]

Spoilers contribute to the climate of suspense that characterizes the weeks during which the new episodes are distributed, and for which the show has become widely popular at an international level. Spoilers also turned out to be relevant because they affect the ways in which fans control the viewing activity in terms of timing and social interactions, mainly via social media. Furthermore, the dynamics related to the management of the "spoiler issue" clearly exemplify the diverse nature of fans' involvement with a show like *Game of Thrones*. If in the case of *Mad Men* spoilers did not represent a real concern for its fans (since the AMC series is about underlying drama that develops at a steady pace), with *Game of Thrones* the shocking and the unpredictable define the narrative system to its core. This means that, for a text of this nature, the role played by fans' predictions and speculations regarding (possible) future occurrences in the storylines emerges as an important trend, since it points out fans' departure from the text and toward virtual places of critical processing, such as online forums and social media conversations, in which fans "are held together through the mutual production and reciprocal exchange of knowledge" (Jenkins, *Convergence Culture* 27).

This dynamic is even more significant for the understanding of the so-called reaction videos phenomenon, through which viewers' reactions to the most horrific and appalling events depicted on the screen have recently developed into a new form of spectacle. By the beginning of 2007, reaction videos started to be disseminated on the Internet and have become very popular on YouTube, especially after the shocking acts represented in *Game of Thrones'* pivotal episode entitled "The Red Wedding" (S03E09). Viewers' reactions to the representation of the savage deeds from this episode were put together in a super-cut that went viral and initiated a sort of a general trend; every most distressing event in the universe of *Game of Thrones* is now accompanied by a collection of reaction videos. In its basic form, a reaction video shows people reacting to an external stimulus of a certain kind. These videos mainly display reactions to screen media, such as movies trailers, TV shows' episodes and videogames. The final goal is to record emotions that are highly pitched, so the scenes within the videos that people are responding to tend to be notably dreadful, gruesome, frightening or exciting. Subsequently, the videos are uploaded onto video-sharing websites such as YouTube, where they can be accessed and viewed widely. In "Embodied Spectatorship and the *Game of Thrones* Reaction Video" (Shacklock), Zoë Shacklock points out the fact that, as a current popular phenomenon, reaction videos are relevant because they make an important statement about the medium of television: "The desire to watch other people is something that television has always exploited. We've always turned to television as a way to gain access to a feeling of community. In its broadcast form, television produces a sense of co-presence, creating a community of viewers held together by their shared participation in the live moment of viewing" (Shacklock 2). In a *New York Times Magazine* article, Sam Anderson stated that reaction videos represent a "fundamental experience of the Internet," since they support, "at a time of increasing cultural difference, the comforting universality of human nature" (Anderson); in this sense, reaction videos symbolize "a shared cultural experience." Reaction videos serve principally two main purposes, and refer to two distinct forms of pleasure that are connected to the act of viewing. In the first place, "in desiring to see other people suffer through the same pain you did, to see them react as you did" (Hudson), reaction videos reinforce a fan community's internal bonds. Even in the age of niche audiences, multiple platforms and personalized viewing schedules, "television is still a significantly shared phenomenon." The idea of shared experiences is still a unifying force that can bring people together, even if at a virtual level; as such, it points out that people respond to the necessity of being part of a group. Second, reaction videos "offer distance and detachment." They build a concrete opportunity "to position oneself as cool and unaffected while others are vulnerable" and can, therefore, become the object of a subtle form of mockery. This double trend clarifies the (seemingly contrasting, and yet essentially human) necessity of individuals to be, at the same time, part of a group and to stand out as unique as well as different from those who tend to react too emotionally.

In the beginning, *Game of Thrones* reaction videos included audience members filming their friends or relatives watching outrageous moments from the show, but the current tendency sees individuals recording their own reactions with webcams. *Game of Thrones* reaction videos are so popular and amusing because the series is capable of generating intense feelings of expectation among its fans. Unpredictability is the show's narrative paradigm, and fans' "quite-often-exaggerated" reactions to turns and twists in the stories con-tribute to cultivate a form of entertainment. Indeed, reaction videos are cre-ated precisely with the expectations that something shocking will occur, and that viewers' responses to that particular event will be worth observing and filming. This attitude exemplifies fans' familiarity with the conventions of the show's narrative, in which unexpected events are instrumental in keeping the audiences' interest always alive. When expectations about fans' responses are met, a condition of gratification is experienced, which also helps to strengthen the sense of community through the confirmation that similar emotions are shared by the members:

- *"If it is a good episode and my friends haven't watched it, I make sure I am with them when they watch it so I can see their reactions. I like doing that but I don't interact with people online about it."* [NZ]
- *"After that people started to put* Game of Thrones *reaction videos on YouTube, I did the same with a friend of mine and I decided to film her reaction to the 'Red Wedding' scene, I couldn't wait!"* [IT]

The corporeal responses of viewers that the *Game of Thrones* reaction videos present—with people shouting, grasping their faces, covering their eyes, jumping out of their seats—indicate a predominant mode of spectatorship that mirrors the enhanced body dynamics of the series itself. This aspect calls attention to the peculiar way through which fans make sense of how they experience the show. The series is famous for the construction of scenes and sequences that incorporate physically stimulating as well as appalling actions; the best way to watch them appears to be through the body, that is, through physical responses that parallel the dynamics of the depicted events.[34] Once again, *Game of Thrones* emerges as a program that promotes a mode of engaging that is directly affected by the features of its visual narrative. In serving the main purpose of reinforcing the sense of community, reaction videos exemplify the importance that fans' practices have in the *"Game of*

---

[34] Shacklock underlines the importance of reaction videos in relation to HBO brand iden-tity and the idea of *Game of Thrones* as quality television:

> *Game of Thrones* is widely known for its particular use of extreme sex and vio-lence: breasts and bottoms, battles and blood. [...] Kim Akass and Janet McCabe note that HBO capitalizes upon the risk-taking connotations of breaking taboos to promote a brand of quality—as they state, "HBO takes control of the illicit and encloses it within its institutional discourse of quality." [...] Reaction videos, then, work perfectly within HBO's brand identity, in which spectacular displays of physicality stand as markers of quality." (Shacklock 4–5)

Thrones experience": they favor fans' interactions and mutual identification, and allow the production of media texts that insert significant parts of the original content of the TV program in a new frame.

"Cosplay" is a further example of fan engagement that articulates fans' willingness to express their passion in a creative way through forms of social gathering. Italian fans referred to this practice as something that is essentially culturally specific because, in explaining the difference in popularity, they drew a comparison between the two cultures. In this sense, the American culture is perceived as more oriented to these forms of entertainment whereas, in Italy, people appear to be less accustomed to participate. Nevertheless, even if the phenomenon does not appear to be very popular in Italy, the fame of *Game of Thrones* seems to be changing this to some extent:

— *"The cosplay is becoming more popular in Italy at the moment."* [IT]
— *"Maybe it is not that popular at the moment but it represents a new opportunity for fans to gather together, in a real way and not just in a virtual space."* [IT]
— *"I think that if they created the concrete chance, even the Italians would start dressing up in costumes!"* [IT]

In this regard, New Zealand fans showed a more practical attitude. They know the phenomenon and their concern is mainly about the amount of money and time that this practice, even if acknowledged as fascinating, requires:

— *"For me it is just something to admire, maybe I'd try the hair styles because they look really great!"* [NZ]
— *"In New Zealand, people would not dress up like the characters and go around, it is not a Kiwi thing!"* [NZ]
— *"People would have to pay a lot of money for the costumes and the accessories."* [NZ]
— *"I am a fan of many TV series and I cannot cosplay for all of them, it is better to admire from a distance."* [NZ]
— *"I think that Halloween would be a good time to dress up as a* Game of Thrones *character, but not more than that."* [NZ]
— *"In terms of new culture, when it comes to cosplay and things like that, I just think that* Game of Thrones *isn't super popular. I think they read it and people talk about it but if there were the mainstream culture with* The Walking Dead *and the new culture, which would be like other aspects of fantasy, I feel that* Game of Thrones *would fall in the middle."* [NZ]

In *Convergence Culture* (2006), Henry Jenkins asserts, "What holds a collective intelligence together is not the possession of knowledge, which is relatively static, but the social process of acquiring knowledge, which is dynamic and participatory, continually testing and reaffirming the group's social ties" (54). This statement can be related to the ways *Game of Thrones'* fans approach the show and deal with the information exchanges that regulate their participation in the online discussions on the show. Fans argue and speculate on the possible advancements of the series' plot by presenting multiple theories about its mysteries. In elaborating these explanations, fans participate in a collaborative process of retrieving and assembling meaningful pieces of information, with the final aim to make reasonable predictions on *Game of Thrones'* future events. But the "solving-the-puzzle" activity is also instrumental in stimulating a teamwork that finds its justification in the pleasure and gratification that team members obtain from taking part in an enlarged system of confrontations and discussions. In addition to this, the cumulative knowledge about the story-world and characters' profiles, as something that belongs to the community itself, emerges as the result of a critical elaboration and deepening of individual insights and observations. From this perspective, each contribution is of importance and finds its validation in the collaborative process of the production of new knowledge about the stories told by *Game of Thrones* (both on written pages and on multiple screens).

This participatory approach aligns with the concept of "centrifugal complexity" as a peculiar narrative conceived in the form of a convoluted network of events and characters, in which a unique center does not exist. Just like *Game of Thrones'* intertwined storylines (with hundreds of characters in a story-world whose vastness exceeds its fictional representation) "push outward," the reception of the show, almost by necessity, surpasses the viewing process to reach out to collaborative forms of understanding and interpretation. As a major tendency, fans discuss theories on online forums regarding future events (mainly, important deaths and killings) and outline alternative lines of development that can account for all the most recent happenings in the plot. The attitude toward spoilers reveals that, at least for some groups of devoted *Game of Thrones* followers, social media discussions can impact (generally in a negative way) on the mode of viewing—hence, this has to be adjusted accordingly. Furthermore, the underlying dynamics of the "reaction videos" phenomenon call attention to the sense of belonging to a community of reference in which members have similar interests and inclinations. In this sense—and in a way that is significantly different from *Mad Men*—*Game of Thrones* emerges as a text that is constructed for being shared and discussed, for being experienced as a common passion within a community of devoted and enthusiastic followers.

The delineation of this scenario appears to be noteworthy in relation to the building of sociality in the current era of convergence, and also because it brings to question the actual role, and the effectiveness, played by transmedia as a strategy employed for impacting on fans' consumption behaviors.

It is worth noticing that what fans brought to the table of conversations had a tenuous connection with the forms of engagement and media options proposed by the official producers for the exploration of *Game of Thrones*' fictitious world. Fans disclosed a general tendency to organize themselves in a system of groups, forums, information websites and alternative sources of *Game of Thrones*-related entertainment that is independent from HBO, and that essentially refers to the core contents—Martin's books, the series' episodes—as the basis for its internal functioning. Indeed, the fact that both New Zealand and Italian fans are deeply interested in the show itself but tend to distance themselves from the items and content that derive from the official producers emphasizes their growing independence in identifying and selecting both the media content of preference and the different venues through which to access it. From this standpoint, official and unofficial media extensions related to the series all become part of a rich context in which trans-media storytelling as a strategy turns into a dynamic concept, a spectrum of possibilities and a plurality of routes that are independently created, selected and discovered, and may not fully follow the dictates of the official producers in the modes of consumption and engagement.

Chapter 5

TRANS-MEDIA STORYTELLING AND FANS' MODES OF ENGAGEMENT: AN OVERVIEW

"Winter is coming."
(Ned Stark, *Game of Thrones*, S01E01)

"If you don't like what is being said, change the conversation."
(Don Draper, *Mad Men*, S03E02)

In the current media climate of growing complexity, the abundance of media products is accompanied by a variety of modes of consumption and engagement. The advancements in technology have allowed individuals to pick out the media content that interests them from a wide range of options and have also provided them with more control over the management of the media experiences they decide to pursue. This relatively rapid change in the habits and behaviors of media users is indicative of broader shifts in the relationship between producers and consumers, as well as a blurring of roles in which "an emphasis on multiplicity emerges as the norm in the creating and viewing of television" (Ross). Therefore, the study of audiences today emerges as a necessity for properly understanding the changes in people's consumption habits and behaviors, and how such transformations interact with the strategies and offers developed by media companies.

Throughout the years, audiences have been studied from diverse perspectives. In particular, studies starting from the 1980s focused more and more on the active role played by audience members in interpreting texts and on the relevance of the environment—especially the domestic environment—on the forms of media consumption. Scholars like David Morley (1980), Charlotte Brunsdon (1981), Dorothy Hobson (1982), Ien Ang (1985) and Elihu Katz and Tamar Liebes (1986, 1993) investigated the process of text interpretation in relation to specific elements such as class, race, gender, culture and ideology. John Fiske (1987) approached the idea of television as a text that is "activated" through the meanings made of its content by active viewers, while in 1986 David Morley shifted his attention to the home as the central setting for an in-depth understanding of the relation between spectators and the medium of television. Along similar lines as Morley's, Stewart M. Hoover, Lynn Schofield Clark and Diane F. Alters (2004) examined the mechanisms of identity construction within the household in relation to the consumption of media products. All these investigations have pointed out the active role played by audience members in the processes of meaning interpretation, as well as the influence of an array of elements on the modalities that define these procedures. In Jay Rosen's words, the people "formerly known as the audience" (2006)—that is, as a passive mass of individuals who were essentially seen as uncritical recipients of media messages—are now officially and fully acknowledged as savvy users of technology and conscious selectors of media content of interest. These people have left the proverbial couch in front of the television set where, for a long time, media producers have (conveniently) pictured them, to experiment with new devices and alternative locations, both within the household and in non-domestic contexts. But, just to be clear, they have not gotten rid of that couch. Nor have they gotten rid of the television set—*definitely* not the television set. The point is that in today's media climate it is up to audiences as users, consumers and sometime-producers to decide when and how, and even why, to go back to the domestic arena to watch the television material they are in the mood for. The couch in front of the television set remains one of the ways in which audience members can enjoy their media experiences, yet the fact that this is only one of the ways—and the fact that even on the couch audiences can engage in multiple, concurrent media experiences—calls attention to the complexity of a landscape in which media forms of consumption intersect and interweave, as well as to the blurring of consumption and production roles that do not lend themselves to easy demarcation.

In the context of convergence, the television industry has been forced to seek out the audience's attention beyond the time of broadcasting, thus opening the doors to the idea of trans-media storytelling (Jenkins, *Convergence Culture*; Scolari; Evans, *Transmedia Television*; Wolf) as a tool to construct enhanced experiences of fictional stories. Trans-media has been grasped as a fascinating prospect and a profitable strategy as well, given its effectiveness in generating a "sentimental bond" with a product that, conveyed in the fashion of a story-world, offers audiences the promise of immersion in its alternative reality. This is more than watching something on a screen; rather, trans-media promises multifaceted ways to *experience* it. And experiences are valuable because they generate feelings that, in turn, are powerful means of connection and involvement. But the efficacy of trans-media strategies in selling experiences that are of concrete fascination for media consumers requires a reassessment—first, from a terminological perspective, and subsequently with regards to the modes of engagement that distinct audiences undertake in relation to specific media objects.

THE "TRANS-MEDIA ISSUE"

Henry Jenkins's definition of trans-media insists on the equivalent relevance of multiple media platforms and entry points in the creation of a "unified and coordinated entertainment experience" (Jenkins, *Convergence Culture*).[1] The "unique contribution" that, according to Jenkins, each medium makes to the story-world within the trans-media network nullifies any sort of hierarchy among texts. Therefore, in this type of scenario, what constitutes proper trans-media extensions (and practices) are those that bring something new and relevant to the advancement of the fictional universe, that enrich its narratives and allow users to acquire new information about the storylines or the characters. This leveling of elements in Jenkins's concept is fundamental to understanding the differences between the architectures of story-worlds conceived in terms of more generic trans-media extensions. Indeed, as Jason Mittell explains,

> Despite the growing ubiquity of trans-media, we need to avoid confusing general trans-media extensions with the more particular mode of trans-media storytelling. Nearly every media property today offers some trans-media extensions, such as promotional websites, merchandise, or behind-the scenes materials—these forms can be usefully categorized as para-texts in relation to the core text, whether a feature film, a videogame, or a television series. As Jonathan Gray has argued in his defining work on the topic, we cannot view any text in our media-saturated age in isolation form its para-texts—for instance, films come pre-framed by trailers, DVD covers, and posters, and once any text enters into cultural circulation, it becomes part of a complex intertextual web. However, we can follow Gray's lead by *distinguishing between para-texts that function primarily to hype, promote, introduce, and discuss a text and those that function as ongoing sites of narrative expansion.* (Mittell 293; my emphasis)

---

[1] See: http://henryjenkins.org/blog/2007/03/transmedia_storytelling_101.html (accessed July 14, 2017).

In the realization of a trans-media cosmos that follows Jenkins's paradigm, the intersection of "ongoing sites of narrative expansion" constitutes the backbone of the structure, and what each of these sites has to offer can be consumed independently of one another, since they all constitute separate entry points to the extended story-world. However, in practice, this is hardly the case. Rather, when it comes to the realization of trans-media worlds, Jenkins's formula emerges as the "ideal" version of those expanded worlds, which, in their actual configuration, are generally made up of promotional para-texts (i.e., of texts that are positioned within a hierarchy of relevance, with the core texts as the primary ones). Once again, it is up to Mittell to point out this distinction between the possible versions of trans-media:[2]

> It is useful to distinguish between Jenkins' proposed ideal of *balanced trans-media*, with no one medium or text serving a primary role over others, with the more commonplace model of *unbalanced trans-media*, with a clearly identifiable core text and a number of peripheral transmedia extensions that might be more or less integrated into the narrative whole, acknowledging that most examples fall somewhere on a spectrum between balance and unbalance. (Mittell; emphasis as in original)

This clarification is not a mere matter of terminology but rather identifies the properties of fictional structures that impact on the ways individuals engage with and become invested in them. Whereas a "balanced trans-media" story-world is supposed to function in a way that equally distributes the intensity of involvement among the nodes of its architecture, in an "unbalanced" one this distribution can easily come out as uneven—in which case it is generally the core text that is given a preference in the modes of engagement. Furthermore, Mittell's distinction helps to keep in mind that "pure" versions of trans-media (as in Jenkins's formulation) are neither the only ones nor are necessarily the most prevalent; hence, the "spectrum" of possibilities between balanced and unbalanced is a realistic frame of reference to take into consideration when analyzing the various features that compose a trans-media construction and, further, investigating how audiences actually engage with story-worlds.

In the case of this comparative research, the notion of "unbalanced trans-media" pertains to both the enlarged architectures of *Mad Men* and *Game of Thrones*. The network of promotional para-texts (i.e., behind-the-scene clips, trailers, videos of interviews with cast and crew, quizzes, posters and

---

[2] With regards to this matter, also see https://transmediajournalism.org/2014/04/21/multimedia-crossmedia-transmedia-whats-in-a-name/ by Kevin Moloney (accessed July 14, 2017) on the definitions of, respectively, multi-media, cross-media and trans-media.

screensavers, applications) that constitute a large portion of the series' official websites are not instrumental in significantly advancing the story of these fictional worlds. On the other hand, elements such as "immersive" videogames that further develop specific storylines (in the case of *Game of Thrones*) or guides for the organizations of parties that allow audiences to re-create a certain atmosphere from the past (in the case of *Mad Men*) are more aligned with the idea of trans-media as a set of potentially independent activities through which these fictional universes are discovered in depth and experienced in diverse ways. As is indicative by the idea of a spectrum, however, there are also texts, platforms and practices within these trans-media configurations that do not fall easily into the category of either para-texts or "pure" trans-media. Thus, the notion of "unbalanced trans-media" emerges as more useful and appropriate with reference to both the universes of *Mad Men* and *Game of Thrones*, not least because followers' modalities of investment disclose an apparent, and remarkable, predilection for the core texts—that is, for the episodes of the TV series—even if these forms of preference are characterized by dynamics that differ substantially.

The idea of augmented universes for audiences to become immersed in implies a predisposition on the part of viewers to dedicating time and energy to these particular media experiences. The nature of this interest can take different forms, but, in general, the level of involvement required by trans-media activities resonates with the degree of passion possessed by fans, that is, by individuals who are profoundly invested in media products. These devoted followers are taken into strong consideration by media producers, since they represent a group of ideal consumers. Driven by a genuine passion that pushes them to constantly look for more content and experiences, these "fanatics"[3] are willing to invest valuable resources in activities that contribute to an ever greater knowledge of the object of their desire. Furthermore, fan communities constitute a driving force for other potential fans, who may end up finding this mixture of excitement and dedication highly contagious. But when it comes to fans' passion, a clarification is necessary, since not all forms of interest and devotion are the same. In particular, given a trans-media world and the forms of investment that it is likely to elicit and support, the difference between "hard-core" and "casual" fans is of interest to this study. Indeed, this distinction does not just represent a matter of theoretical speculation; it also emerges as a founding principle for the functioning of trans-media as a productive strategy:

---

[3] The word "fan" was originally an abbreviation of this term.

Trans-media storytelling presents a world to be traversed and explored
[…] As a whole, these experiences position the hard-core fan as "the
main hero" who drives the plot forward through their own spatial
movements. Just as a character in a videogame discovers a new part of
a world by entering a new level or area, a hard-core fan discovers a new
part of a trans-media world by purchasing a new novel, movie, or comic
book. As hard-core fans navigate the nuances of a world, casual fans
can imagine a vast expanse (hyper-diegesis) without having to explore it
further. It is the same logic as many role-playing games: hard-core fans
can get the full experience by following every side mission, while casual
fans can focus on the main quest and see how the primary story unfolds.
In any case, a trans-media creator should evoke the spatial dimensions
of a world in order to encourage hard-core fans to "play" within it.
(Smith)

The targeting of "hard-core" fans is meant to ensure media producers find a
positive response to the media content they are offering. Indeed, it is highly
likely that these people will engage with the multiple layers of a reality as
complex as the one represented by the "hyper-diegesis" (Hills, *Fan Cultures*).
Furthermore, the idea that "a trans-media creator should extend the spatial
dimensions of a world in order to encourage hard-core fans to 'play' within it"
calls attention to the assumption—on the producers' side—that these devotees
might eventually decide to get creative so as to factually contribute to the
enlargement of the trans-media architecture through the production of user-
generated content. This practice stands as a distinctive trait of the behavior of
a "hard-core" fan; original creativity, particularly in the form of fan art and
fan fiction, is seen as the natural outcome of the intense passion that drives
fan behavior.

But this begs a question: with reference to the differentiation between
"hard-core" and "casual" fans, is trans-media more effective as a strategy
for *developing* fans' investment in a given story-world or is it more useful for
reinforcing and *preserving* the interest that fans already have? I believe that it
is possible to argue that the two things are not necessarily mutually exclu-
sive. Nevertheless, the findings of this comparative research point out the fact
that the category of "hard-core" fans does not appear to identify the majority
of people within the fan base. As a matter of fact, when it comes to audience behaviors in terms of modes of engagement, "casual" fans are those
who emerge as more numerous, which has important implications for what
producers and researchers may assume about audience practices. What this

means for trans-media is that, as a general trend, a "full experience" of a trans-media cosmos does not represent the *typical* fan experience, which, on the contrary, comes out as more partial, contained and dependent, among other things, on the cultural context of viewing.

If we accept "fan" as a concept that refers to a category of consumers who display degrees of intensity in the ways they express dedication and involvement, then it is worth noting that focus group participants themselves emphasized the difference between fans who tend to be "more" and "less" active. This means that they displayed awareness of an existing distinction between "hard-core" and "casual" fans (even if they did not employ this exact terminology). The predominant notion in scholarship is that *real* fans are individuals so passionate about something—a movie, a graphic novel, a fictional character, a TV show—that they ultimately feel the necessity to express their devotion by engaging in creative activities that lead to user-generated content (mainly fan art or fan fiction). But with regards to this concept, people appear to have a different perception of the matter.

In 2015, Mélanie Bourdaa from the University of Bordeaux Montaigne (Pessac, France) and Javier Lozano Delmar from the Loyola University (Seville, Spain) carried out a qualitative research study on French and Spanish fans and non-fans of *Game of Thrones*, with the final goal being to "understand how European viewers perceive themselves as fans and what it means for them to be fans" (Bourdaa and Delmar). Their analysis revealed that "French and Spanish fans are not keen on defining themselves as fans, and when they do, they do not engage in many of the activities that are associated with the performance of fandom, such as creating fan artworks" (Bourdaa and Delmar). With reference to the production of user-generated content, a limited production of this sort on fans' side calls attention to the necessity to reevaluate the characteristics of fan behavior, so as "to better understand if fans' roles are actually related to user-generated content" (Bourdaa and Delmar). This is also a useful reassessment when it comes to think in terms of trans-media practices and the people who might be *more inclined* to respond to them. On the other hand, with regards to the attitudes toward "fan status," it is worth noting that both Italian and New Zealand participants employed this label to define their attachment to the series, but they also indicated significant differences in the various levels of involvement and dedication. Indeed, the acknowledgment of the distinction between fans who are, in participants' words, "more" or "less" involved did not prevent these people from considering themselves as *real fans too*, and for reasons that are not necessarily accountable for the practices listed by scholars as "proper" fan behavior. This raises the question of what specific characteristics our focus group participants draw on, explicitly or implicitly, when they think of themselves as fans of *Mad Men* or *Game of Thrones*.

In the first place, what was resonant with the focus group participants was the belief that they were following TV shows that are different from other series. This fact becomes a source of pride, as well as a unifying element within the communities of reference. In addition to this, participants described their commitment to the shows in terms of their (a) consistent viewing of the episodes; (b) clear knowledge and understanding of the characters' personalities and plot developments[4] and (c) a desire to discuss the show with close friends and other fans, both offline and online.[5] These types of activities legitimated the participants' consideration of themselves as authentic fans of the series, even if this set of practices does not comprise playing immersive videogames, writing fan fiction, making fan art works inspired by the storylines, purchasing merchandise or dressing up as the characters in organized re-enactments such as cosplay performances.

At this point, if we go back to the "trans-media issue" in the terms that have been previously outlined, it becomes apparent that Jenkins's original idea of a network of media elements to be experienced as having equal relevance and attractive power does not represent the actual approach of the majority of audience members committed to a program. In this sense, it is precisely the "unbalanced trans-media" model that, in terms of the dynamics it outlines, supports the reasons provided by our focus group participants for illustrating the nature of their interest and attitudes. Furthermore, the preference granted to the core texts justifies fans' limited investment in the other elements of the expanded model, and calls attention to the spectrum of possibilities that the status of "being a fan" refers to. But there is actually more to this matter. In fact, the core texts *in themselves* can support forms of involvement that either direct the interest of fans toward the "logic of trans-media" or suppress that interest from developing in this direction. From the conversations with the participants, this aspect emerged as the most significant difference between *Game of Thrones* and *Mad Men*. Moreover, in terms of the crucial findings of this study, it points to the existence of a meaningful connection between a text's features and the ways it is watched, interpreted and, ultimately, experienced by its enthusiastic followers.

---

[4] For *Game of Thrones*, the "extraordinariness" (in fans' words) of the program emerges as also connected to an out-of-the-ordinary viewing behavior, in the sense that the show succeeds in instilling in its fans a pressing desire, an imperative want for new content. For *Mad Men*, on the other hand, the uniqueness of the series is represented by its multiple layers of meaning (both from a visual and content perspective) that require fans' patience and dedication throughout the advancement of the stories.

[5] Point (c) refers more to the fans of *Game of Thrones* than to ones of *Mad Men*.

MAD MEN VERSUS *GAME OF THRONES*: HOW NARRATIVE COMPLEXITY MATTERS FOR TRANS-MEDIA

Mad Men fascination originates from the contrasting emotions that arise in its fans when they encounter a universe that is perceived as distant but also relatable and familiar, especially in terms of the existential problems that characterize the lives of the characters. The fictional protagonists of *Mad Men* are flawed individuals, with both good and bad qualities, who are forced to deal with the fact that the world they inhabit is radically, and inevitably, changing. As central and essential as this concept is for the creator of the series Matthew Weiner, the idea of change becomes integral to the development of the program's storylines. It informs the relation between historical recreation and fictional events, and allows the development of a discourse mainly centered on the human perception of time and on the range of emotions evoked by the impact of historical shifts on personal aspirations, needs and accomplishments. *Mad Men* is a series whose narrative displays a type of complexity that can be classified as "centripetal": "actions and characters [are pulled] inward toward a gravitational center, establishing a thickness of backstory and character depth that drives the action. The effect is to create a story-world with unmatched depth of characterization, layers of backstory, and psychological complexity building on viewers' experiences and memories over the program's numerous seasons" (Mittell 222–23). This internal organization of the fictional content—in terms of themes, characters' profiles and plot development—affects fans' approach to the mode of viewing *as well as* to the type of involvement in the show.

Mad Men—as in the media text itself—stands as a complex object that does not necessarily require the presence of additional material (like trans-media extensions) in order to be fully comprehended and experienced. Indeed, fans of the series from both nationalities plainly stated that Weiner's creation elicits forms of consumption and engagement that constantly move toward the text's "gravitational center," along the direction of a set of analytical practices aimed at discovering the depth of its story-world (made up of underlying references, visual clues and multiple meanings) *within* the narrative, rather than outside of it. In this sense, it is significant that *Mad Men* fans proposed comparisons with *Game of Thrones* to explain the peculiar differences in the ways that the programs' narratives tend to impact on fans' involvement in distinct media texts. Even if they were probably unaware of the type of complexities that distinguish the narratives of the two shows,[6] fans' descriptions and explanations

---

[6] Focus group participants never employed the expressions "centripetal/centrifugal complexity" to describe the organization of the textual attributes of, respectively, *Mad Men* and *Game of Thrones*.

of the dynamics that identify their modalities of viewing and investment come out as aligned with the "internal movements" that characterize the narrative progressions of *Mad Men*. This is the reason why the comparison between *Mad Men* and *Game of Thrones* in the terms presented by fans is so valuable for this comparative research. On the one hand, it reveals the existence of a significant relation between textual properties and specific modes of consumption and, on the other, it functions as a sort of "wake-up call" for trans-media by drawing attention to those fictional stories that, even if transformed into enlarged story-worlds via trans-media extensions, are, in the end, *less likely* to be experienced through these additional immersive tools.

If *Mad Men* is a series that does not appear to gain any particular additional benefit from the media extensions that populate its extended structure, when it comes to *Game of Thrones*, some elements of its enlarged architecture play a highly relevant role in the ways fans become invested. On this basis, it is possible to conclude that, as far as trans-media goes, not all series are equal: some are a better fit than others.

The mixture of genres, the complexity of the storylines (numerous and varied, and all intertwined), the nuances that characterize characters' personalities, the events that develop in unpredictable ways, the action and the constantly "over-the-top" drama, and the combination of violence and sex in a form of televisual representation that constantly pushes the limits of what is admissible on screen—these elements together create the fascination that *Game of Thrones* exerts on its audiences. In a way that emerges as more intensified and visually striking than the sense of uneasiness that *Mad Men* induces in its followers, *Game of Thrones* excels in promoting conflicting feelings in its fans. The alternation of images that show the magical and the supernatural with scenes and sequences that are filled with terrifying acts of realistic violence and disturbing sex becomes a source of both attraction and horror, and provides the viewing of the show with the controversial label of "guilty pleasure" spectacle. The series consistently challenges its fans—and fans do love it for this—by testing their ability to tolerate the more and more upsetting depictions of human brutality, while at the same time this amplification has made the recurring seasons of the program extremely popular. In this sense, the "*Game of Thrones* experience" turns out to be something different from the *Mad Men* one. Characterized by a form of "centrifugal complexity," "in which the ongoing narrative pushes outward, spreading characters across an expanding story-world" (Mittell 222–23), the HBO show builds a narrative dimension that keeps expanding along a direction that, from the center, moves toward peripheral areas, not exactly identifiable with fixed boundaries, since the centrifugal movement constantly pushes those boundaries further away, so as to redefine the vastness of this convoluted universe. In a way that is similar to the geographical expansion of the world of the Seven Kingdoms, the fandom of *Game of Thrones* has been growing through the years (and the show's seasons) and has profoundly contributed to the increasing popularity of the program. This is mainly due to the fact that *Game of Thrones* is a media text that serves the dynamics of interaction and collaboration peculiar to fan communities. The show is conceived in the form of a puzzle to be solved, is highly controversial in the assortment of its depictions and displays an alternative reality that provides fans with a great deal of material that supports immersion in a parallel world. Furthermore, the constellation of external activities that inform the management of the viewing process ("spoiler issue," online posts, distribution of reaction videos) calls attention to the relevance that the outside—as in, the context in which the series is received and processed—plays in the experience that fans have of *Game of Thrones*. The outcome of all this is that, when it comes to fictional narratives characterized by a type of complexity that can be identified as "centrifugal," the resources offered by trans-media can be expected to be *more taken into account* than in the case of stories, such as *Mad Men*, that do not encourage the same forms of interpretation of and connection with the text.

WHERE DO WE GO FROM HERE?

The substantial differences found between *Mad Men* and *Game of Thrones* enthusiasts in experiencing the fictional texts validates the comparative aspect of this study in terms of shows. Due to their peculiar narrative attributes, *Mad Men* and *Game of Thrones* tend to elicit diverse modes of fan engagement that, in turn, impact on fans' interest and attraction toward the set of possibilities offered by trans-media.

As for the elements that refer to the cultures of origin, the meaningful dissimilarities between Italians and New Zealanders call attention, in the first place, to the ways the series are watched. The results from the quantitative analysis outline trends that suggest Italian audiences are more committed than New Zealanders during the time of viewing. Indeed, the former display a greater tendency to watch the programs by themselves and without engaging in parallel activities than the latter. This can be explained by taking into account the fact that Italians tend to watch the series in the original language (as admitted during the focus group discussions), either with or without subtitles. With this premise, it can be assumed that watching a TV show in a foreign language requires more attention and dedication than watching the same program in the native idiom. In this sense, Italians' choice is exemplary of viewers' desire to access the core texts in their original form. While for New Zealanders this fact, for obvious reasons, does not represent an element of concern, overcoming the language barrier for Italians constitutes a significant indicator of the propensity to make the viewing experience "as genuine as possible"; watching the shows in English, then, is not a caprice but a sense of commitment to and respect for the aesthetic identity of the texts. On the other hand, New Zealanders' more pronounced inclination toward the practice of binge-watching calls attention to a viewing procedure that, in the first place, appears to be *less* demanding for this group than for the Italians—at least in terms of attention and concentration required to understand and follow the dialogue. Moreover, through the practice of binge-watching the basic components of the texts are assembled together in new blocks of narrative: the fictional journey is not contained any longer within the time of the single episode but is rather reorganized in the time and space of the context of consumption. From this perspective, it is reasonable to state that the effort in the viewing on the side of the New Zealand public consists mainly in creating a "mega-episode" text through the process of binge watching, whereas for the Italian viewers the effort is essentially language-based.

On the basis of these and other findings detailed in this project, I believe that it is in these attitudes that the real power of fans today lies: in the concrete possibilities of claiming for themselves media encounters that can satisfy their thirst for awe and excitement as well as for compassion and empathy; in the awareness of being able to choose alternative approaches and venues of consumption that might emerge as more captivating and involving; and in the distinctiveness that characterizes their actively interpretive mechanisms of appreciating the texts and engaging with their expanded story-worlds. All of these modes, as this study has uncovered, are necessarily affected by specific cultural codes and ideologies, but, precisely for this reason, they are of grave relevance for a proper understanding of the relation between audiences and media products.

APPENDIX I

SURVEY QUESTIONS

QUESTIONS ABOUT THE TV SHOWS:

1. *Have you watched all the episodes of the seasons of the show so far?*
   - *Yes*
   - *No*
2. *If you answered no: How many episodes have you watched so far?*
   - *Between 0 and 10*
   - *Between 10 and 30*
   - *Between 30 and 60*
   - *Between 60 and 100*
3. *Do you watch the show's episodes live on television?*
   - *Never*
   - *Rarely*
   - *Sometimes*
   - *Often*
   - *Always*
4. *If you do not watch the episodes live, how do you watch them?*
   - *On DVR/TiVo*
   - *On DVDs*
   - *On iTunes*
   - *Through legal streaming services*
   - *Other (please specify)*
5. *What time do you usually prefer watching the show's episodes?*
   - *In the morning (6 a.m.–12 p.m.)*
   - *In the afternoon (12 p.m.–6 p.m.)*
   - *In the evening (6 p.m.–11 p.m.)*
   - *During the night (11p.m.–6 a.m.)*

6. *On which platform(s) do you tend to watch the show more often?*

	Never	Rar ely	Sometimes	Often	Always
TELEVISION					
LAPTOP					
TABLET					
MOBILE					
PHONE					
SCREENS					
IN PUBLIC					
SPACES					
OTHER					

7. *Do you watch three or more episodes of the series in a single sitting?*
   - *Never*
   - *Rarely*
   - *Sometimes*
   - *Often*
   - *Always*
8. *When you watch the show, is it usually the only thing you are doing? (Tick all that apply)*:
   - *I do not do anything else while watching the show*
   - *I engage in domestic tasks (cooking, cleaning, etc.)*
   - *I chat with people offline and / or online*
   - *I chat with people offline and / or online about the episode I am watching*
   - *I surf the net*
   - *I play games*
   - *Other (please specify)*
9. *When you watch the show, are you usually engaging with others? (Tick all that apply)*:
   - *No, I watch the episodes by myself*
   - *Yes, I watch the episodes with my family at home*
   - *Yes, I watch the episodes with my friends at my house*
   - *Yes, I watch the episodes with my friends at someone else's house*
   - *Yes, I watch the episodes with my family / friends who are somewhere else through synchronous viewing on one or more technological devices*
   - *Yes, I post comments on the official Facebook / Twitter pages of the series about the episode I am watching*
10. *Do you produce media content related to the series? Choose from the list:*
    - *Mash-ups*
    - *Music videos*

- *Clips*
- *Web-based animations*
- *Photo collages / Posters*
- *Other (please specify)*

11. *Do you distribute media content related to the series? Choose from the list:*
    - *Mash-ups*
    - *Music videos*
    - *Clips*
    - *Web-based animations*
    - *Photo collages / Posters*
    - *Other (please specify)*

12. *How often do you produce media content related to the series?*
    - *Once a week or more*
    - *Once a month*
    - *Every now and then*

13. *Do you share or post the content you produce related to the series? If so, how often?*
    - *No*
    - *Once a week*
    - *Once a month*
    - *Every now and then*

14. *Do you visit the show's official website?*
    - *Never*
    - *Rarely*
    - *Sometimes*
    - *Often*
    - *Always*

15. *Do you visit other sites about the show?*
    - *Never*
    - *Rarely*
    - *Sometimes*
    - *Often*
    - *Always*

16. *Have you ever downloaded some of the show's applications or played the online games?*
    - *Never*
    - *Rarely*
    - *Sometimes*
    - *Often*
    - *Always*

17. *Which applications and which games? Choose from the list* [for *Game of Thrones*]
    - *Game of Thrones Companion*
    - *Game of thrones Wiki*

- *Game of Thrones Trivia with Friends*
- *A Game of Thrones Reference*
- *News for GoT*
- *iQuiz for Game of Thrones*
- *Ice & Fire*
- *Join the Realm*
- *Game of Thrones: Ascent*
- *Other (please specify)*

18. *Which applications and which games? Choose from the list* [for *Mad Men*]
    - *Mad Men Cocktail Culture*
    - *Mad Men Job Interview*
    - *Ultimate Fan Game*
    - *Which Mad Men Character Are You Now?*
    - *Which of Don's Women Are You?*
    - *Name That Secretary Photo Quiz*
    - *Other (please specify)*

19. *Do you follow the updates and/or post comments on the official Facebook/Twitter pages of the TV series?*
    - *No, I do not*
    - *Yes, I follow them but I do not post anything*
    - *Yes, I follow them and I also post comments*

20. *If you answered yes: how often do you usually post your comments?*
    - *Several times a day*
    - *Two/three times a week*
    - *Once a week*
    - *Once every two or three weeks*
    - *Once a month*

21. *Have you ever bought any of the following items: books, DVDs and/or other merchandise that is associated with the show's name?*
    - *Yes, I have*
    - *No, I have not*

22. *Which items in particular? Choose from the list* [for *Game of Thrones*]
    - *Game of Thrones DVDs*
    - *Books*
    - *Dolls*
    - *Figurines*
    - *Mugs and Glasses*
    - *Posters and Maps*
    - *T-shirts*
    - *Cards*
    - *Lunchboxes*

- *Exercise books*
- *Paperweights*
- *Magnet sets*
- *Other (please specify)*

23. *Which items in particular? Choose from the list* [for *Mad Men*]
    - *Mad Men DVDs*
    - *Mad Men: The Illustrated World*
    - *The Fashion File: Advice, Tips and Inspiration from the Costume Designer of Mad Men*
    - *Sterling's Gold: Wit and Wisdom of an Ad Man*
    - *Mad Men CDs*
    - *Mad Men Barbie Dolls*
    - *Other (please specify)*

24. *Do you participate in forum discussions about the show?*
    - *Never*
    - *Rarely*
    - *Sometimes*
    - *Often*
    - *Always*

25. *If you answered yes: How often do you participate in these discussions?*
    - *Several times a day*
    - *Two / three times a week*
    - *Once a week*
    - *Once every two or three weeks*
    - *Once a month*

26. *In addition to the viewing of the TV series, have you also read any of George Martin's books?* [for *Game of Thrones* only]
    - *Yes, I have*
    - *No, I have not*

27. *If you said yes, did you start reading the books before or after the TV series aired?*
    - *I started reading the books before the series aired*
    - *I started reading the books after the series aired*

28. *Is there anything else you would like to say regarding the way(s) you watch the show?*

GENERAL QUESTIONS ABOUT THE PEOPLE

1. *What is your gender?*
   - *Male*
   - *Female*
   - *Transgender*

2. *What is your ethnic group?*

- *European*
- *Maori*
- *Asian*
- *Pacific Island*
- *Middle Eastern*
- *African*
- *Other*
- *Prefer not to say*

3. *What is your age?*
    - *19 or under*
    - *20–29*
    - *30–39*
    - *40–49*
    - *50–59*
    - *60–69*
    - *70 and over*
    - *Prefer not to say*

4. *Which city or town do you live in?*

5. *As of right now, what is the highest degree or level of education that you have completed?*
    - *Less than high school*
    - *Some high school, no diploma*
    - *Graduated from high school—diploma or equivalent*
    - *Bachelor's Degree*
    - *Bachelor (Honors) Degree*
    - *Master's Degree*
    - *Doctorate Degree*
    - *Prefer not to say*

6. *What is your occupation?*

7. *To investigate the results of this questionnaire, we are organizing focus groups on your favorite TV series!! Groups will take place in the city of Auckland. Would you be willing to participate?*

APPENDIX II

FOCUS GROUP TOPICS

The focus group sessions that took place, respectively, in Milan (Italy) and Auckland (New Zealand) with fans of both shows were instrumental to an in-depth investigation of the general trends—in terms of viewing habits and modes of engagement—that emerged from the participants' responses to the online surveys. The focus group discussions were structured in such a way to allow participants to express freely their feelings, preferences and interests regarding their favorite show, from the viewing process to the practices reflecting forms of investment in the show as well as social interactions, to the main reasons at the basis of their devotion for the program.

I started the moderation of the sessions by asking specific questions regarding the modality of viewing of the episodes, ranging from the choice of viewing platform to the preferred time and conditions for watching the show, mainly in terms of

– Choice of the best context;
– Company of other people *versus* viewing in solitude;
– Engagement in parallel activities related/or not related to the series during the viewing time

Participants gradually began to engage with each other about the dynamics of these habits and explain the motivations at the heart of their choices; they also provided relevant information regarding the nature of their passion for and attachment to the TV series under discussion. In particular, during the focus groups with the Italian fans of the shows, participants spent some time discussing their reasons for choosing (main trend) or not choosing to watch the original version of the programs, a topic that also allowed a conversation to develop about the problems related to the Italian broadcast of international media products (specifically, with reference to the *Mad Men* case).

The central part of the session was entirely dedicated to the forms of involvement in additional practices, beyond the viewing one, that constitute fundamental elements of the trans-media logic employed to construct and present the fictional universes of the shows. In the first place, I asked participants questions regarding their actual knowledge of the series' transmedia architectures and, subsequently, I moved the conversation to the level of engagement that this type of strategy is capable of eliciting. During this phase, participants had the chance to express their points of view on the production and distribution logics that pertain to the policies of media corporations, as well as on the current media scenario from the perspective of their role as active users *and* critical viewers of media products. In this context participants also discussed online fan communities and distinctions between fan-generated content and material provided by official sources.

The final part of the group discussion focused on the textual elements of the series—in terms of production values, aesthetics, construction of the narratives, characters' profiles and themes—that represent the main sources of attraction and excitement for fans in watching and talking about their beloved shows and the emotions that they are capable of generating.

BIBLIOGRAPHY

Anderson, Sam. "Watching People Watching People Watching." *New York Times Magazine*, November 25, 2011.

Ang, I. *Watching "Dallas": Soap Opera and the Melodramatic Imagination*. London: Methuen, 1985.

Askwith, Ivan D. *Television 2.0: Reconceptualizing TV as an Engagement Medium*. Cambridge: Massachusetts Institute of Technology, 2007.

Atkinson, Sarah. "The Performative Functions of Dramatic Communities: Conceptualizing Audience Engagement in Transmedia Fiction." *International Journal of Communication* 8 (2014): 2201–19.

Beail, Linda, and Lilly J. Goren. *Mad Men and Politics: Nostalgia and the Remaking of Modern America*. New York: Bloomsbury, 2015.

Beaton, Elizabeth. "Female Machiavellians in Westeros," in *Women of Ice and Fire; Gender, Game of Thrones, and Multiple Media Engagement*, edited by Anne Gjelsvik and Rikke Schubart, 203. New York: Bloomsbury, 2016.

Bennett, Lucy, and Paul Booth, eds. *Seeing Fans: Representations of Fandom in Media and Popular Culture*. New York: Bloomsbury, 2016.

Booker, M. Keith, and Bob Batchelor. *Mad Men: A Cultural History*. Lanham, MD: Rowman & Littlefield, 2016.

Bourdaa, Mélanie, and Javier Lozano Delmar. "Case Study of French and Spanish Fan Reception of *Game of Thrones*," in European Fans and European Fan Objects: Localization and Translation, edited by Anne Kustritz, special issue, *Transformative Works and Cultures* 19 (2015). doi.org/10.3983/twc.2015.0608.

Bratich, Jack Z. "Amassing the Multitude: Revisiting Early Audience Studies." *Communication Theory* 15, no. 3 (2005): 242–65.

Brevik-Zender, Heidi. "'A Place Where We Ache to Go Again': Fashion and Nostalgia in *Mad Men*," in *Lucky Strikes and a Three Martini Lunch: Thinking about Television's Mad Men*, edited by Danielle M. Stern, Jimmie Manning and Jennifer C. Dunn, 27–43. Newcastle upon Tyne: Cambridge Scholars, 2012.

Bronfen, Elisabeth. *Mad Men, Death and the American Dream*. Zurich: Diaphanes, 2016.

Bruns, Axel. "Towards Produsage: Futures for User-Led Content Production." *Proceeding of the 5th International Conference on Cultural Attitudes towards Technology and Communication*. School of Information Technology, 2006.

Brunsdon, Charlotte. "'Crossroads' Notes on Soap Opera." *Screen* 22, no. 4 (1981): 32–37.

Caldwell, John Thornton. "Convergence Television: Aggregating Form and Repurposing Content in the Culture of Conglomeration," in *Television after TV: Essays on a Medium in Transition*, edited by L. Spigel and J. Olsson, 41–74. Durham, NC: Duke University Press, 2006.

Caldwell, John Thornton. *Production Culture: Industrial Reflexivity and Critical Practice in Film and Television*. Durham, NC: Duke University Press, 2008.

Campbell, Jessica. "The Good Place That Cannot Be: Visual Representations of Utopia on *Mad Men*," in *Mad Men, Women and Children*, edited by Heather Marcovitch and Nancy E. Batty, 91–104. Lanham, MD: Lexington Books, 2012.

Carpentier, Nico. *Media and Participation: A Site of Ideological-Democratic Struggle*. Bristol: Intellect, 2016.

Carpentier, Nico. "New Configurations of the Audience? The Challenges of User-Generated Content for Audience Theory and Media Participation," in *The Handbook of Media Audiences*, edited by Virginia Nightingale, 190–212. Hoboken, NJ: John Wiley, 2011.

Carpentier, Nico, Kim Christian Schroder and Lawrie Hallett. *Audience Transformations: Shifting Audience Positions in Late Modernity*. New York: Routledge, 2014.

Chin, Bertha, and Lori H. Morimoto. "Towards a Theory of Transcultural Fandom." *Participations: Journal of Audience & Reception Studies* 10, no. 1 (2013): 92–108.

Ciasullo, Ann M. "Not a Spaceship, but a Time Machine: *Mad Men* and the Narratives of Nostalgia," in *Lucky Strikes and a Three Martini Lunch: Thinking about Television's Mad Men*, edited by Danielle M. Stern, Jimmie Manning and Jennifer C. Dunn, 14–26. Newcastle upon Tyne: Cambridge Scholars, 2012.

Clarke, M. J. *Transmedia Television: New Trends in Network Serial Production*. New York: Bloomsbury, 2013.

Codeluppi, Vanni. *Che cos'è la pubblicità?*. Rome: Carocci, 2001.

Codeluppi, Vanni. *Il potere della marca. Disney, McDonald's, Nike e le alter*. Turin: Bollati Boringhieri, 2001.

Codeluppi, Vanni. *Lo spettacolo della merce. I luoghi del consumo dai passages a Disney World*. Milan: Bompiani, 2000.

Colvile, Robert. "Game of Thrones: A Show That Breaks the Golden Rules of Television," *Telegraph*, May 2012. http://www.telegraph.co.uk/culture/tvandradio/game-of-thrones/9280766/Game-of-Thrones-a-show-that-breaks-the-golden-rules-of-television.html (accessed July 14, 2017).

Couldry, Nick. "The Necessary Future of the Audience … and How to Research It," in *The Handbook of Media Audiences*, edited by Virginia Nightingale, 213–29. Malden, MA: Wiley-Blackwell, 2011. ISBN 9781405184182.

Curtin, Michael. "Matrix Media," in *Television Studies after TV: Understanding Television in the Post-Broadcast Era*, edited by Graeme Turner and Jinna Tay, 9–19. London: Routledge, 2009.

Dadlez, E. M. "Arya Stark as a Rough Hero," in *The Ultimate Game of Thrones and Philosophy: You Think or Die*, edited by Eric J. Silverman and Robert Arp, vol. 105, 10. Chicago: Open Court, 2016.

Das, R. "Converging Perspectives in Audience Studies and Digital Literacies: Youthful Interpretations of an Online Genre." *European Journal of Communication* 26, no. 4 (2011): 343–60.

Davies, Madeleine. "Game of Boners: This Is Torture Porn," Jezebel, 2013. https://jezebel.com/game-of-boners-this-is-torture-porn-504821180 (accessed July 14, 2017).

De Castella, Tom. "*Game of Thrones*: Why Does It Inspire Such Devotion among Fans?" *BBC News*, March 2013. http://www.bbc.com/news/magazine-21856915 (accessed July 14, 2017).

Dell, C. "'Lookit that Hunk of a Man': Subversive Pleasures, Female Fandom and Professional Wrestling," in *Theorizing Fandom: Fans, Subculture and Identity*, edited by C. Harris and A Alexander. Cresskill, NJ: Hampton, 1998.

Dockterman, Eliana. "*Game of Thrones'* Woman Problem Is about More than Sexual Assault," *Time*, June 2015.

Duffett, Mark. *Understanding Fandom: An Introduction to the Study of Media Fan Culture*. New York: Bloomsbury, 2013.

Dwyer, Tim. *Media Convergence*. Maidenhead: Open University Press, 2010.

Edgerton, Gary R. "The Selling of Mad Men: A Production History," in *Mad Men: Dream Come True TV*, edited by Gary R. Edgerton, 3–24. New York: Bloomsbury, 2010.

Evans, Elizabeth. "Character, Audience Agency and Transmedia Storytelling." *Media, Culture & Society* 30, no. 2 (2008): 197–213.

Evans, Elizabeth. *Transmedia Television: Audiences, New Media, and Daily Life*. New York: Routledge, 2011.

Farrell, Hannah. "Not a 'Jackie', Not a 'Marilyn': *Mad Men* and the Threat of Peggy Olson," in *Mad Men, Women, and Children*, edited by Heather Marcovitch and Nancy E. Batty, 33. Lanham, MD: Lexington Books, 2012.

Ferraro Guido. "Entrare nel www," In *Il dolce tuono. Marca e pubblicità nel terzo millennio*, vol. 32, edited by Marco Lombardi, 169–89. Milano: FrancoAngeli, 2000.

Ferraro, Guido. *La pubblicità nell'era di Internet*. Roma: Meltemi, 1999.

Field, Andy. *Discovering Statistics Using IBM SPSS Statistics*. Newbury Park, CA: Sage, 2013.

Fiske, John. *Television Culture*. London: Methuen, 1987.

Flood, Alison. "George R.R. Martin Defends *Game of Thrones'* Sexual Violence," *Guardian*, May 6, 2014. https://www.theguardian.com/books/2014/may/06/george-rr-martin-game-of-thrones-sexual-violence (accessed July 14, 2017).

Freeman, M. *Historicising Transmedia Storytelling: Early Twentieth-Century Transmedia Story Worlds*. New York: Routledge, 2016.

Gambarato, Renira, R. "How to Analyse Trans-Media Narratives?" in *Baltic Film and Media School Screen Studies*, edited by Andres Joesaar, 14–24. Tallinn: Tallinn University Press, 2012.

Genz, Stephanie. "'I Am Not Going to Fight Them, I Am Going to Fuck Them': Sexist Liberalism and Gender (A)Politics in *Game of Thrones*," in *Women Of Ice and Fire: Gender, Game of Thrones and Multiple Media Engagement*, edited by Gjelsvik and Schubart, 243–66. New York: Bloomsbury, 2016.

Gillan, Jennifer. *Television and New Media: Must-Click TV*. New York, Routledge, 2011.

Gjelsvik, Anne. "Unspeakable Acts of (Sexual) Terror As/In Quality Television," in *Women of Ice and Fire: Gender, Game of Thrones and Multiple Media Engagement*, edited by Gjelsvik and Schubart, 57–78. New York: Bloomsbury, 2016.

Gjelsvik, Anne, and Rikke Schubart. Introduction to *Women of Ice and Fire: Gender, Game of Thrones and Multiple Media Engagements*, 1–17. New York: Bloomsbury, 2016.

Goggin, Gerard. "Going Mobile," in *The Handbook of Media Audiences*, edited by Virginia Nightingale, 128–46. Hoboken, NJ: John Wiley & Sons, 2011.

Gray, A. "Audience and Reception Research in Retrospect: The Trouble with Audiences," in *Rethinking the Media Audience: The New Agenda*, edited by P. Alasuutari, 22–37. London: Sage, 1999.

Gray, J., C. Sandvoss and C. L. Harrington. "Introduction: Why Study Fans?" in *Fandom: Identities and Communities in a Mediated World*, edited by J. Gray, C. Sandvoss and C. L. Harrington, 1–16. New York: New York University Press, 2007.

Green, Joshua, and Henry Jenkins. "Spreadable Media: How Audiences Create Value and Meaning in a Networked Economy," in *The Handbook of Media Audiences*, edited by Virginia Nightingale, 109–27. Malden, MA: Wiley-Blackwell, 2011.

Grodal, Torben. *Moving Pictures: A New Theory of Film Genres, Feelings, and Cognition.* Oxford: Oxford University Press, 1999.

Gunning, Tom. "Moving Away from the Index: Cinema and the Impression of Reality," reprinted in *The Film Theory Reader: Debates and Arguments*, edited by M. Furstenau, 255–69. London: Routledge, 2010.

Gunter, Barrie, and David Machin. *Media Audiences*. London: SAGE, 2009.

Hall, Stuart, "Encoding/Decoding," in *Culture, Media, Language*, Stuart Hall, D. Hobson, A. Lowe and P. Willis, 128–38. London: Hutchinson, 1980.

Harrington, C. Lee, and Denise D. Bielby. "Introduction: New Directions in Fan Studies." *American Behavioral Scientist* 48, no. 7 (2005): 799.

Harrington, C. Lee, and Denise D. Bielby. *Soap Fans: Pursuing Pleasure and Making Meaning in Everyday Life*. Philadelphia: Temple University Press, 1995.

Harris, Cheryl, and Alison Alexander. *Theorizing Fandom: Fans, Subculture, and Identity.* New York: Hampton Press, 1998.

Hietalahti, Jarno. "Tyrion's Humor," in *The Ultimate Game of Thrones and Philosophy: You Think or Die*, edited by Eric J. Silverman and Robert Arp, vol. 105, 28. Chicago: Open Court, 2016.

Hills, Matt. "Cult TV, Quality and the Role of the Episode/Programme Guide," *Contemporary Television Series*, 2005, 190–206.

Hills, Matt. "The Expertise of Digital Fandom as a 'Community of Practice' Exploring the Narrative Universe of Doctor Who." *Convergence* 21, no. 3 (2015): 360–74.

Hills, Matt. *Fan Cultures*. London: Routledge, 2002.

Hobson, Dorothy. *Crossroads: The Drama of a Soap Opera*. London: Methuen, 1982.

Hoover, Stewart M., et al. *Media, Home, and Family*. London: Psychology Press, 2004.

Hudson, Laura. "What's Behind Our Obsession with *Game of Thrones* Reaction Videos," *Wired*, May 6, 2014. https://www.wired.com/2014/06/game-of-thrones-reaction-videos/ (accessed July 14, 2017).

Itzkoff, Dave. "George R.R. Martin on *Game of Thrones* and Sexual Violence," *New York Times*, May 2014. https://artsbeat.blogs.nytimes.com/2014/05/02/george-r-r-martin-on-game-of-thrones-and-sexual-violence/?_php=true&_type=blogs&_r=0 (accessed July 14, 2017).

Jancovich, M. "Cult Fictions: Cult Movies, Subcultural Capital and the Production of Cultural Distinctions." *Cultural Studies* 16 (2002): 306–22.

Jenkins, Henry. *Convergence Culture: Where Old and New Media Collide*. New York: New York University Press, 2006.

Jenkins, Henry. "The Cultural Logic of Media Convergence." *International Journal of Cultural Studies* 7, no. 1 (2004): 33–43.

Jenkins, Henry. "Interactive Audiences? The Collective Intelligence of Media Fans." *New Media Book* (2002): 157–76.

Jenkins, Henry. "Revenge of the Origami Unicorn: The Remaining Four Principles of Trans-media Storytelling," 2009. http://henryjenkins.org/blog/2009/12/revenge_of_the_origami_unicorn.html (accessed October 14, 2017).

Jenkins, Henry. *Textual Poachers: Television Fans and Participatory Culture*. London: Routledge, 1992.

Johnston, Susan. "Grief Poignant as Joy: Dyscatastrophe and Eucatastrophe in *A Song of Ice and Fire*." *Mythlore* 31, no. 119 (2012): 141.

Juluri, Vamsee. *Becoming a Global Audience*. Hyderabad, India: Orient Blackswan, 2004.

Katz, Elihu, and Tamar Liebes. "Interacting with 'Dallas': Cross Cultural Readings of American TV." *Canadian Journal of Communication* 15, no. 1 (1990): 45–66.

Kinder, Marsha. *Playing with Power in Movies, Television, and Video Games: From Muppet Babies to Teenage Mutant Ninja Turtles*. Berkeley: University of California Press, 1991.

Larsson, Mariah. "Adapting Sex: Cultural Conceptions of Sexuality in Words and Images," in *Women of Ice and Fire: Gender, Game of Thrones and Multiple Media Engagement*, edited by Anne Gjelsvik and Rikke Schubart, 17–38. New York: Bloomsbury, 2016.

Lehman, Katherine. "More Than Just a "Marilyn": Peggy, Joan and the Single Working Woman of the 1960s," in *Lucky Strikes and a Three Martini Lunch: Thinking about Television's Mad Men*, edited by Jennifer C. Dunn, Jimmie Manning and Danielle M. Stern, 159–76. Newcastle upon Tyne: Cambridge Scholars, 2012.

Levene, H. "Robust Tests for Equality of Variances," in *Contributions to Probability and Statistics: Essays in Honor of Harold Hotelling*, edited by I. Olkin, 278–92. Palo Alto, CA: Stanford University Press, 1960.

Liamputtong, Pranee. *Focus Group Methodology: Principle and Practice*. Thousand Oaks, CA: Sage, 2011.

Liebes, Tamar, and Elihu Katz. *The Export of Meaning: Cross-Cultural Readings of Dallas*. Oxford: Oxford University Press, 1990.

Liebes, Tamar, and Elihu Katz. "Patterns of Involvement in Television Fiction: A Comparative Analysis." *European journal of communication* 1, no. 2 (1986): 151–71.

Liebes, Tamar, and Elihu Katz. "Six interprétations de la série Dallas." *Hermès* 1, no. 11–12 (1993): 125–44.

Livingstone, S. M. "From Family Television to Bedroom Culture: Young People's Media at Home," in *Media Studies: Key Issues and Debates*, edited by E. Devereux, 302–21. Thousand Oaks, CA: Sage, 2007.

Lunt, Peter, and Sonia Livingstone. "Rethinking the Focus Group in Media and Communications Research." *Journal of Communication* 46, no. 2 (1996): 79–98.

MacDonald, Sara, and Andrew Moore, eds. *Mad Men: The Death and Redemption of American Democracy*. Lanham, MD: Lexington Books, 2016.

Marc, David. "Mad Men: A Roots Tale of the Information Age," in *Mad Men: Dream Come True TV*, edited by Gary R. Edgerton, 226–38. London: I.B. Tauris, 2011.

Marcovitch, Heather, and Nancy E. Batty, eds. *Mad Men, Women and Children*. Lanham, MD: Lexington Books, 2012.

Marotte, Mary Ruth. "Not a 'Jackie,' Not a 'Marilyn': *Mad Men* and the Threat of Peggy Olson," in *Mad Men, Women and Children*, edited by Heather Marcovitch and Nancy E. Batty, 33–44. Lanham, MD: Lexington Books, 2012.

Mattenson Mundt, Alisa, and Elizabeth Ward. "Inside the Mind of 'Don Draper': Abuse and Its Legacy, a Portrait of the 'As If' Personality," in *Lucky Strikes and a Three Martini Lunch*, edited by Danielle M. Stern, Jimmie Manning and Jennifer C. Dunn, 108–16. Newcastle upon Tyne: Cambridge Scholars, 2012.

Mittell, Jason. *Complex TV: The Poetics of Contemporary Television Storytelling*. New York: New York University Press, 2015.

Moloney, Kevin. "Multimedia, Crossmedia, Transmedia ... What's in a Name?" *Transmedia Journalism* 21 (2014).

Morley, David. *Family Television: Cultural Power and Domestic Leisure*. London: Routledge, 2005.

Morley, David. *The Nationwide Audience: Structure and Decoding*. London: British Film Institute, 1980.

Muller, F., and J. Hermes. "The Performance of Cultural Citizenship: Audiences and the Politics of Multicultural Television Drama." *Critical Studies in Media Communication* 27, no. 2 (2010): 193–208, doi: 10.1080/15295030903550993.

Napoli, Philip M. *Audience Evolution: New Technologies and the Transformation of Media Audiences.* New York: Columbia University Press, 2011.

Nightingale, Virginia, ed. *The Handbook of Media Audiences.* Malden, MA: Wiley-Blackwell, 2011.

Pande, Rukmini. "Squee from the Margins: Racial/Cultural/Ethnic Identity in Global Media Fandom," in *Seeing Fans: Representations of Fandom in Media and Popular Culture,* edited by Lucy Bennett and Paul Booth, 209–21. New York: Bloomsbury, 2016.

Perryman, N. "Doctor Who and the Convergence of Media. A Case Study in Transmedia Storytelling." *Convergence: The International Journal of Research into New Media Technologies* 14, no. 1 (2008): 21–39.

Poniewozik, James, "The Time Machine: How *Mad Men* Rode the Carousel of the Past into Television History," 2017. http://time.com/mad-men-history/ (accessed July 14, 2017).

Rosen, Jay. "The People Formerly Known as the Audience," in *Participation and Media Production: Critical Reflections on Content Creation,* edited by Nico Carpentier and Benjamin De Cleen, 163–67. Newcastle: Cambridge Scientific Publishers, 2008.

Ross, Sharon Marie. *Beyond the Box: Television and the Internet.* Malden, MA: Wiley-Blackwell, 2008.

Sandvoss, Cornel. *A Game of Two Halves: Football Fandom, Television and Globalization.* London: Routledge, 2003.

Sandvoss, Cornel. *Fans: The Mirror of Consumption.* Cambridge: Polity, 2005.

Sandvoss, Cornel. "Reception," in *The Handbook of Media Audiences,* edited by Virginia Nightingale. Malden, MA: Wiley-Blackwell, 2011.

Schubart, Rikke. "Woman with Dragons: Daenerys, Pride, and Postfeminist Possibilities," in *Women of Ice and Fire: Gender, Game of Thrones and Multiple Media Engagements,* edited by Anne Gjelsvik and Rikke Schubart, 105–29. New York: Bloomsbury, 2016.

Scolari, Carlos Alberto. "Trans-Media Storytelling: Implicit Consumers, Narrative Worlds, and Branding in Contemporary Media Production." *International Journal of Communication* 3 (2009): 586–606.

Semprini, Andrea. *La marca dal prodotto al mercato, dal mercato a la società.* Milano: Lupetti, 1996.

Semprini, Andrea. *Lo sguardo semiotico: Pubblicità, stampa, radio.* Milano: FrancoAngeli, 1990.

Semprini, Andrea, and Musso, Patrizia, "Dare un senso alla marca," In *Il dolce tuono. Marca e pubblicità nel terzo millennio,* vol. 32, edited by Marco Lombardi, 43–66. Milano: FrancoAngeli, 2000.

Sender, Katherine. *The Makeover: Reality Television and Reflexive Audiences.* New York: New York University Press, 2012.

Shacklock, Zoë. "Embodied Spectatorship and the Game of Thrones Reaction Video," *Game of Thrones: An International Conference,* University of Hertfordshire, September 6–7, 2017.

Silverman, Eric J. "Horrifying Violence, Gratuitous Sex, and the Truth," in *The Ultimate Game of Thrones and Philosophy: You Think or Die,* edited by Eric J. Silverman and Robert Arp, 209–16. Chicago: Carus, 2017.

Simons, Nele. "Audience Reception of Cross- and Transmedia TV Drama in the Age of Convergence." *International Journal of Communication* (2014): 2220–39.

Smith, Aaron. *Trans-Media Storytelling in Television* 2.0, 2009. http://sites.middlebury.edu/mediacp/2009/06/17/the-art-of-worldbuilding/ (accessed December 8, 2017).

Snedecor, George W., and Witiiam G. Cochran. *Statistical Methods*, 8th edn. *Ames: Iowa State Univ. Press Iowa* 54 (1989): 71–82.

Spigel, Lynn, and Jan Olsson. *Television after TV: Essays on a Medium in Transition.* Durham: Duke University Press, 2004.

Spiro, John-Paul, and Peter Augustine Lawler. "*Mad Men*'s Selective Nostalgia and Uncertain Progress," in *Mad Men: The Death and Redemption of American Democracy*, edited by Sara MacDonald and Andrew Moore, 60. Lanham, MD: Lexington Books, 2016.

Stern, Danielle M., Jimmie Manning and Jennifer C. Dunn, eds. *Lucky Strikes and a Three Martini Lunch: Thinking about Television's Mad Men.* Newcastle upon Tyne: Cambridge Scholars, 2012.

Stern, Marlow. "*Game of Thrones*' Most WTF Sex Scene: Nicolaj Coster-Waldau on Jaime Lannister's Darkest Hour," *Daily Beast*, April 2014.

Stoddart, Scott F., ed. *Analyzing* Mad Men: *Critical Essays on the Television Series.* Jefferson, NC: McFarland, 2011.

Sullivan, John. *Media Audiences: Effects, Users, Institutions, and Power.* Thousand Oaks, CA: Sage, 2013.

Tasker, Yvonne, and Lindsay Steenberg. "Women Warriors from Chivalry to Vengeance," in *Women of Ice and Fire: Gender, Game of Thrones and Multiple Media Engagement*, edited by Anne Gjelsvik and Rikke Schubart, 171–92. New York: Bloomsbury, 2016.

Tenderich, Burghardt, and Jerried Williams. *Transmedia Branding: Engage Your Audience.* Nierstein, Germany: EIMO, 2014.

Terranova, T. "Free Labor: Producing Culture for the Digital Economy." *Social Text* 18, no. 2 (2000): 33–58. doi: 10.1215/01642472-18-2_63-33.

Tufte, Thomas. *Living with the Rubbish Queen: Telenovelas, Culture and Modernity in Brazil.* Bloomington: Indiana University Press, 2000.

Turner, Graeme. *British Cultural Studies: An Introduction.* East Sussex: Psychology Press, 2003.

Webster, J. G. "The Audience." *Journal of Broadcasting & Electronic Media* 42, no. 2 (1998): 190–207.

Wells-Lassagne, Shannon. "Adapting Desire: Wives, Prostitutes, and Smallfolk," in *Women of Ice and Fire: Gender, Game of Thrones and Multiple Media Engagement*, edited by Anne Gjelsvik and Rikke Schubart, 39. New York: Bloomsbury, 2016.

White, Mimi. "Mad Women," in *Mad Men: Dream Come True TV.*, edited by Gary R. Edgerton, 154. New York: Bloomsbury Publishing, 2010.

Williams, Zoe. "*Game of Thrones* Despises You. And That's Why You Love It," *Guardian*, April 2016. https://www.theguardian.com/tv-and-radio/2016/apr/20/game-of-thrones-despises-you-thats-why-you-love-it (accessed July 14, 2017).

Wilson, Julia C., and Joseph H. Lane Jr. "Is *This* the Traditional American Family We've Been Hearing So Much About?: Marriage, Children, and Family Values in *Mad Men*," in *Mad Men, Women, and Children*, edited by Heather Marcovitch and Nancy E. Batty, 77–90. Lanham, MD: Lexington Books, 2012.

Witchel, Alex. "*Mad Men* Has Its Moment," *New York Times*, June 22, 2008.

Wolf, Mark J. P. *Building Imaginary Worlds: The Theory and History of Sub-creation.* London: Routledge, 2012.

"Worst Characters on TV: Our Least Favorite Characters from 'Revenge,' 'The Good Wife,' 'The Walking Dead' and More." *Huffington Post*, May 24, 2012. https://www.huffingtonpost.com/2012/05/24/worst-characters-on-tv_n_1540267.html (accessed August 8, 2017).

INDEX

www.ingramcontent.com/pod-product-compliance
Lightning Source LLC
Chambersburg PA
CBHW020003290326
41935CB00007B/285